Advance Praise for

BECOMING UNSILENCED

As a survivor, I am moved by the courage of those who are turning their pain into purpose and using their voices to shine a light on the Troubled Teen Industry. Meg reminds us of the strength that comes from speaking our truth and fighting for justice! Proud of you, babe!

—**Paris Hilton,** entrepreneur, philanthropist, and survivor

Meg Appelgate is a rare individual. I have been working in this field for over 30 years helping people who have been manipulated and coerced, and I have therefore met thousands of people who have experienced events similar to Meg's. What makes Meg stand out is her insightfulness, her personal strength, devotion and tenacity. While many people in her shoes have understandably just enough energy to heal and try to make it through the day, Meg has drawn from personal strength to move mountains, to get the word out, and to help others feel more protected and supported. Meg has also gone on to engage in the uphill battle and often very frustrating and disheartening goal of changing public perception and evolving how our legal system addresses this so that people have the potential to finally be protected from those who treat teens as expendable and as a means to make a fraudulent living.

Thanks to Meg for her openness and bravery that threads itself through her memoir, and through her life's work.

—**Rachael Bernstein,** educator, therapist, author, cult and re-acclamation specialist, board member of ICSA, and host of the weekly podcast, *IndoctriNation*

Meg Appelgate will no longer stay quiet about a billion-dollar industry that sold abuse as therapy and kept her locked away for much of her adolescence. Read this book to understand why tough-love residential treatment does not help troubled teens—and what must be done to prevent these businesses from preying on vulnerable families.

—**Maia Szalavitz,** author of several books including *Help At Any Cost: How the Troubled-Teen Industry Cons Parents and Hurts Kids,* and contributing opinion writer for the New York Times

At once a memoir, a cautionary tale and an important call to action, *Becoming UNSILENCED* gives voice to all the teens abused in a very troubling industry. An important and compelling read for understanding coercion and cultic environments.

—**Sarah Edmondson,** author of *Scarred: The True Story of How I Escaped NXIVM, the Cult That Bound My Life,* and host of the podcast *A Little Bit Culty*

Becoming UNSILENCED is an excellent, in-depth look at the Troubled Teen Industry and the hidden abuses it entails. As a survivor, I saw a lot of parallels between what I experienced in the extreme Children of God cult, and what Meg went through. From my perspective as a scholar of cults, the author makes valid parallels between the kinds of identity-breaking indoctrination used by entities like cults and the military, and what children who enter the Troubled Teen Industry are forced to survive. This book also provides an excellent map and resources to those readers needing to deconstruct and understand their own experiences as young people growing up under religious group control.

—**Daniella Mestyanek Young,** author of *Uncultured*, and scholar of cults, extreme groups, and extremely bad leadership

Meg Appelgate's heartfelt book adds to the increasing number of well written memoirs that document the misdiagnosis and mistreatment that characterize the Troubled Teen Industry. It is particularly significant because of Meg's important role as the founder of UNSILENCED, which has provided a voice and a meeting place for the industry's victims and because the book tells not only Meg's story, but also the story of her parents whose love for their daughter made them vulnerable to the industry's marketing and false promises.

—**Phil Elberg**, attorney and Troubled Teen Industry expert

The power in *Becoming UNSILENCED* is not only Meg Appelgate's candor but how she connects her personal experiences to universal themes shared by thousands of survivors of the Troubled Teen Industry (TTI). She describes unethical clinical methods encountered during a six-month hospital stay in Idaho and three years of reeducation at a Montana program.

This intimate account offers parents and policy makers a glimpse inside the "black box" of the TTI. Her reflections come to life with insights given from several perspectives—how she perceived things then, how she learned to silence her discomfort and pain, how she understands such methods now, and how she finds healing through naming and articulating what she experienced.

This memoir is much more than a story about institutionalized abuse. It documents Meg's lived experiences as a key foundation stone for Unsilenced, the visionary activist group she co-founded in 2022. Appelgate offers readers an example of how adult TTI survivors continue to heal through advocacy. *Becoming UNSILENCED* tells a story about what pushes so many to speak out, lifting voices together to sustain the social movement against institutionalized abuse.

—**Marcus Chatfield,** TTI researcher and historian

Becoming
UNSILENCED

Surviving and Fighting the Troubled Teen Industry

MEG APPELGATE

Memoir Dedication

To my beloved parents, Dick and Beth Gochnauer, whose unconditional love and ongoing support are the bedrock of my resilience and grit. Despite the pain of our shared past, your commitment to fighting injustice and standing by me inspires me every day.

To my cherished children—Spencer, Jackson, Harper, and Bentley—you are my "why." You are my greatest teachers, my guiding lights, and the reason I fight to create a better world. Thank you for filling my life with love, strength, and purpose.

To my incredible husband, your unwavering support, love, and tireless behind-the-scenes efforts at home have made everything possible. Thank you for believing in me.

Contents

Foreword

BY JANJA LALICH, PH.D

Despite the many years I have worked in the field of cults and coercion, it wasn't until the mid-2000s that I first learned about the Troubled Teen Industry (TTI) when I was contacted by Marcus Chatfield. He told me that at age 16, his parents had been advised by a school counselor to put him in Straight, Inc., one of the most notorious programs in the TTI. I mentored Marcus, who soon after went on to university. His research project was later published and is an important contribution to this field: *Institutionalized Persuasion: The Technology of Reformation in Straight Incorporated and the Residential Teen Treatment Industry.*

Through Marcus, in 2012, I was invited to give a keynote speech at a weekend conference of Survivors of Institutional Abuse (SIA), convened aboard the historic ocean liner, Queen Mary, docked in Long Beach, California. Amidst the fabulous Art Deco interior designs, I met and listened to dozens of survivors and learned about their horrific experiences in various TTI programs here in the States and sometimes on remote islands. I was absolutely mortified that I knew so little about this well-organized and well-funded mistreatment of young people.

At the time, I was a sociology professor at California State University, Chico. After that weekend, I asked the students in my classes, "Does anyone know someone who was kidnapped in the night out of their bedroom and taken to a behavior-modification program?" Just about every student raised their hand. I thought, *Wow! How did I miss this?*

Thus began my heightened interest in educating myself on the special features of being a TTI survivor. I saw a clear connection to what I know about cultic systems of abuse and their aftereffects. However, there were some significant aspects that stood out among TTI survivors. A most obvious one, of course, is that when adults "join" (that is, get recruited into) a cult or cult-like organization, they are adults. Whereas, in the case of the TTI, a teenager is regularly mysteriously abducted in the middle of the night by goons with handcuffs and the startled and confused teen has no idea where they are going. The experience comes as a total shock. And for those who are taken to a facility by a parent, here also, the teen has absolutely no say in the matter.

Another key difference is that TTI programs not only sequester their victims, but they are essentially inmates. Yes, it is difficult to leave a cult because of the psychological manipulation and indoctrination; but in most cases, the cult member is not literally being held against their will.

Some TTIs, like the one described in these pages by Meg Applegate, may tell you, "There are no locks on these doors." But where are you going to go? Quite consistently, TTI facilities are located in remote areas. So, imagine this: You're a teenager who is terrified. Most likely, you've already been abused and harmed while in the program. You are definitely freaked out. You have no money. You have no phone. No possessions. You know that if you call your parents, they will just turn you in because they've been convinced that this program is the last resort for "saving" you from your "bad behavior."

It is precisely that confinement that is the hallmark of these programs and that also becomes the hallmark of the aftereffects of the experience and the type of recovery necessary afterwards. The feeling of inescapability experienced in a cult is largely "in your mind"—in that you are psychologically trapped. Whereas in TTI programs, you are not only psychologically trapped, indeed, you are actually physically trapped—and that sense of inescapability can stay with you for years.

Combine that with the stage of maturation teenagers find themselves in. When you are a teen, you are trying to figure out who you are, who you want to be. It's a time of exploration. However, when in a TTI program, another personality is drilled into you. A personality that is, in most cases, a hostile, aggressive, and paranoid personality—because that's what these programs teach and that's who you need to become in order to "graduate." So, bear in mind that the human brain is not fully developed until you are 25 years old, which means that everything that happens to you in your younger years has a huge impact. If there's trauma, if there's abuse—be it physical, sexual, emotional, or psychological—it all goes very deep because, in part, you don't have the resources to manage or cope with it. In that way, survivors of TTI programs are very similar to individuals who were born and raised in a cult, in that they also lack independent choice and undergo developmental stages that are not their own.

I have found that working with TTI survivors tends to raise some of the most difficult challenges I've encountered in my work. Understandably, they don't want to go into therapy because they were told that the attack therapy they were subjected to (originating in Synanon) was good for them. They are skeptical of people educating them because everything they were taught was wrong. TTI survivors tend to be filled with mistrust, and rightly so.

Thus, I have profound respect for Meg Appelgate's ability to conquer those demons and misconceptions. She has gone on to form the organization, Unsilenced, which, more than any other organization, has had visible success in fighting the TTI. This is nothing short of remarkable, given everything she's been through. Meg knows how to run an organization, keep it focused and keep it healthy. As a member of the board of directors of my own nonprofit, Meg has taught me so much and I'm thrilled and honored to observe her wisdom, energy, and passion. Because of Meg and all that I've learned about the TTI in the past decade, I added a section in the newly revised 2023 edition of my book *Take Back Your Life: Recovering from Cults and Abusive Relationships*. The new section includes history and analysis of the industry and survivors' personal accounts.

Meg's parents also have my utmost respect. Having been present when her father gave the presentation that is included in this book, I can tell you that it was one-of-a-kind, intensely heartfelt, and simply fantastic. One of the least talked-about aspects of the TTI is how parents are conned and "brainwashed." Desperate parents are taken advantage of and exploited by educational consultants who recommend the programs (some of the same consultants also get kickbacks), while the children are typically misdiagnosed and sorely abused. Naturally, parents are not as abused as the teens are; yet, this is certainly another travesty in the world of the TTI that must be stopped.

In *Becoming UNSILENCED: Surviving and Fighting the Troubled Teen Industry*, Meg brilliantly educates readers about the harms and risks of the TTI. Not only does she know her stuff, but Meg also knows herself. I've rarely seen a survivor go through all that she experienced and end up with such strength and clarity at her core. Meg is a survivor, yes. And she is also a warrior. But more than that, Meg is a beacon of light and hope that one day hopefully soon the Troubled Teen Industry will be a thing of the past; one day it will be recognized society-wide as a huge mistake that has endangered and harmed countless teens and bamboozled countless parents.

—Janja Lalich, Ph.D.
CEO, Lalich Center on Cults and Coercion
Professor Emerita of Sociology

Introduction

ENOUGH IS ENOUGH

I was sent away at the age of fifteen, and it took 18 years for me to wake up. All those years to comprehend the sheer magnitude of what I had been through at such a young age.

My entire high school career was spent away from home, against my will, in two Troubled Teen Industry (TTI) programs.

It started with six months in complete lockdown at Intermountain Hospital in Boise, Idaho. From there, I transferred to Chrysalis, a therapeutic boarding school in Eureka, Montana where I spent the next three years.

Three and a half years where I missed normal teenage things.

Three and a half years where I spent birthdays alone, or in isolation.

Three and a half years where I missed key milestones like getting a driver's license, attending school dances, and first loves and heartbreaks.

Three and a half years of isolation, institutionalization, and abuse.

I was also adopted shortly after birth and I was dealing with that trauma, as well as being an undiagnosed autistic who desperately mirrored and masked myself to appear neurotypical and blend in.

I went so far as to create different identities during my institutionalization in an effort to survive and distance myself from my experience. I went by Mary in the hospital because they insisted on calling me by my legal name, which I've never gone by. I told them I went by Meg because my maiden name is Mary Elizabeth Gochnauer, and those were my initials, M-E-G. They didn't care. They called me Mary, anyway. It didn't feel like real life, so I just let it happen.

Then at Chrysalis, the program owner's name was Mary too, so it got confusing. I told them my middle name was Elizabeth, and they were like, "How about Lizzy?" So I went by Liz.

It seemed easier if bad things happened to Lizzy or Mary, not Meg.

Some of you may be wondering what I mean by a Troubled Teen Industry program. That term may be unfamiliar, unless you are one of the 120,000–200,000 youth who find themselves sent to one every year.

Troubled Teen Industry programs are a network of powerful and punitive congregate care facilities that claim to help at-risk youth by way of behavior modification techniques and other non-evidence-based practices. Youth exiting these facilities usually leave calling themselves a "survivor," and the facilities they attended they call their "program."

For a decade and a half after leaving Montana, if you asked me about my experiences in these places, I'd tell you that they were the best thing that ever happened to me. I'd tell you that I came home a stronger, better person, that I'd learned so much about myself and the world around me. I'd sing the praises of these "schools" and claim they truly saved my life—until people I attended these places with started dying.

The first death was a Chrysalis "sister" of mine named Cindy.

Cindy was incredibly smart. One of the first memories I have of her is sitting on the floor in the main house in Chrysalis, at a very young age—I think she was only 12—and she's holding an advanced book of chemistry. It was obviously not something you read for fun. She was extremely academic and a free spirit. She also dealt with chronic pain and chronic disorders like Ehlers-Danlos syndrome, which I also have. I was told she also, like me, went on to experience some very abusive relationships that exacerbated her already existing trauma.

Had she, like myself, moved from an adolescence of abuse and coercion to surrounding herself with abusive and coercive relationships? While the official cause of death was a cocaine overdose, there are many who believe that the circumstances leading up to her death, and her death itself, were very suspicious and could've involved foul play.

By the second death, I had already decided to write this book.

I was in a salon watching my tween-age daughter, Spencer, get a "wolf haircut," whatever that is, while my youngest daughter, Harper, was about to get a lot of her hair cut off because she refused to take care of it or brush it. My husband, Ben, and I had to split parenting tasks that day just to make it through. Ben had our two boys, Bentley and Jackson, at home attempting to make dinner.

You know, it was a typical weekend day with four kids.

I checked Facebook and saw Cristen had passed away. I started sobbing; I had spent so much time with Cristen in Chrysalis, most of my time actually. While we didn't talk anymore, there is still that bond you have with people you shared so much time with.

I don't remember why she had been sent to Chrysalis to begin with. We all had possible explanations, and sometimes those overlapped. Sometimes it was undiagnosed learning disorders, sometimes it was family issues, sometimes it was drugs, or a dozen other excuses for parents to outsource their child-raising struggles.

With Cristen's death I felt like I had reached a threshold for the amount of pain I could tolerate.

Our body holds trauma inside of it. As the CEO of Unsilenced (which you will hear much more about) hearing about sexual, physical, and emotional abuse was a daily reality for me by this point, but due to my years of undiagnosed autism and trauma, I developed a coping mechanism of intellectualizing all of my feelings instead of feeling them. This allowed me not to feel anything too deep, unless I chose to; somehow I had managed to remain objective and keep my cool around others. This one hurt, though; this one I couldn't hide my reaction to.

I don't believe that your body will let you feel things until you are capable of handling all of the emotions that come flooding back.

Now, this may not be the most accepted viewpoint on parenting, but I try not to filter big emotions in front of my children. If I need to cry, I cry. If I'm frustrated, I don't hide it—I announce I'm frustrated. I try and model for them how to handle big emotions, and more importantly, that it is acceptable to have big emotions. With that said, I do not cry often, and my kids know this.

Now I was sitting there with the feeling that I literally swallowed something gigantic. It was stuck in my chest and there was nothing I could do about it. I just had to let it out. It was an enough-is-enough kind of feeling. I just started bawling my eyes out.

The hairdresser stopped mid-cut to look at me shocked. Spencer turned to face me and asked, "Mom are you okay?" I continued to cry and muttered, "I will be, but an old Chrysalis sister just died. Another one."

The third death I heard about was Michelle.

She was one of the early Chrysalis girls, the "OG's." I always viewed her as the favorite of Kenny and Mary, the husband-and-wife team who co-owned the facility. I assumed that meant she had an easier time of it than the rest of us.

I never saw her struggle while she was in the program, but she seemed to be struggling quite a bit at the end.

Before she left us, she was having some kind of erratic behavior where she posted dozens of times a day on Facebook, rants that didn't seem to make much sense at the time:

I'd rather die than think of the hauntings of your abuse. But rather it be you.. Because you abused me.

While some of the language was hard to parse, the passion behind it was clear.

Please pray that I can open my own boarding school ... I want to protect and uplift you. I want to tell you [you're] beautiful everyday ... a place where you decide what you want to do ....

I pray for Chrysalis to shut down by the state of Montana for [their] abuse. I hope you lose every dollar you ever earned. Your abuse will be shown before the world. You disgusting human beings ....

I didn't know if she was waking up or breaking down. I know now those are often the same things, and it requires incredible strength, perseverance and support to make it through to the other side.

Reading through these posts after the fact filed me with guilt. *What if I had seen these?* I wondered. *Would I have been able to prevent this?* Could I have prevented this if I been there to support Michelle, and let her know she wasn't alone?

Survivor's guilt is real, and something we need to pay attention to, because TTI program attendees have been conditioned to always take the blame. We are taught that everything is in our control and everything is our fault. It is essential in our healing to know where our influence begins, and where it ends.

This isn't the first time I had seen that type of behavior from a Chrysalis girl after leaving Chrysalis. There are so many of us that struggle with the trauma and that comes out in various ways.

For the better part of my life since leaving Chrysalis, close to 20 years, I have gone back and forth between very conflicting positions. I would put certain pieces together and then realize, *Oh my god, I feel like there's more to it.* I probably didn't even realize I was waking up at first. It was a process of resistance and then more awareness. I would hold onto a little piece of resistance and then experience fuller awareness, and so on.

It was a slow process to be able to own what had happened to me. My waking up process was accelerated around this time when I watched Paris Hilton's documentary, *This is Paris.* In the documentary, she recounts what happened to her when she was taken in the middle of the night to her programs, and what her abductors had said to her: "We can do this the easy way or the hard way."

I had never heard from someone else's mouth—except another Chrysalis girl—that they had been abducted.

I remember thinking, *How could that be possible? How could her abductors have said the exact same thing to her that they did to me? We went to different "boarding schools."*

As I watched, I realized that there was a community of people like me who had been adversely affected by the Troubled Teen Industry. I found out it was an industry, with entrenched political connections to protect its own interests, and it was spread all over the world. Furthermore, this network of "boarding school" programs existed for the sole purpose of trying to change who children are. By using behavior modification techniques and punishments that would be illegal for parents to use on their own children in most states, these programs existed for the sole purpose of housing minors and profiting from child abuse.

I did not go to a boarding school; I went to a program. I vowed to never use that term again.

Up until this point, I thought I had been able to talk about my past freely and had accepted that my childhood was less than ideal, but every time I talked about it there wasn't any emotion connected to it. I thought that meant I was over it, but holy shit was I wrong.

When I started crying watching *This Is Paris,* it was one of those intense and ego-leveling cries that happen when a connection within yourself is made. *Oh shit, I was abused. I was manipulated.* I remember saying that over and over in my head, and with every repetition it connected deeper and deeper inside me and began to attach itself to my memories.

Now I know that not only are kids dying in TTI facilities, but they're also dying for decades afterwards because of what they went through.

Where was the accountability?

The only people who seemed to experience any potential remorse or recriminations were the parents, who had made the decision to send their kids away when they were desperate enough to follow the advice of educational consultants or other "experts." Parents and survivors were the only demographics who seemed to be suffering, as families splintered apart and lost members whether due to suicide, addiction or estrangement. The TTI's themselves are intact, despite having wreaked havoc on an entire country for decades.

How could we continue to let them get away with it?

To further confuse matters, Chrysalis girls continued to post in our groups about how great their experiences were, and it felt so invalidating. They didn't think what happened to them was abusive. They would say the same things I used to say about how Chrysalis was the best thing that ever happened to them. And the fact that our sisters were dying, some by their own hand, is that just random? Did they think that just happens sometimes?

Finally, I had a conversation with one of my really dear friends, Shay, who was also a Chrysalis sister. I said, "Do you think the things that happened at Chrysalis were okay?"

"No," she replied. "It was abuse."

"What? Why haven't we talked about this?"

She said, "Because you weren't ready. I've known since I was there, but I've been waiting to be able to talk to you about it."

That's when it clicked: *Oh my gosh, I was brainwashed.*

In the same way that a child who is sexually abused doesn't necessarily know that it's abuse, if it's done at a certain time in their life and development, I assumed my experience had happened to everyone. I generalized: "Well, my parents put me here, so it's obviously not abuse." It's the same thing as, "My uncle did that thing to me, so it's obviously not abuse." You have these rationalizations as a child for things you don't understand.

The TTI leaves you with limited options. When confronted by trauma we hear about four options—flight, fight, fawn or freeze. Flight didn't work because if you ran away from Chrysalis you would not be allowed back. You would be sent instead to other "less ideal" programs they dangled in front of you as scary alternatives to the "heaven" they provided.

Then you have to figure out what to do with your life. I witnessed this many times. The girls who ran were never allowed back, and I saw a few who ran, and ended up homeless. I saw that happen.

In the beginning, I was in the fight response. I went up against the male owner, Kenny, with all that I was worth, but I lost every time. I was outmatched for my age, and I had none of the power.

Fawning was tricky. You can't lie too low because those girls aren't liked either. It is said they don't "work the program." You had to have a specific temperament for Kenny to like you; you couldn't threaten his ego in any way. You had to stroke it, but not overstroke it—if you did that, you were a kiss ass. It was either walk this tightrope or be stuck in a house for a long time with people who don't make you feel loved or cared about.

All that was left after that was to freeze, which is what I did for half of my life. My development was arrested by the TTI and it led to abusive relationships with narcissists and two failed marriages. It led to mental health challenges such as anxiety, panic attacks, and agoraphobia.

It also led to more physical health challenges that you can likely believe. I have had my appendix, spleen, gallbladder, and tonsils removed. I have Hashimoto's disease, Ehlers-Danlos syndrome (EDS), Mast Cell Activation Syndrome (MCAS), and Postural Orthostatic Tachycardia Syndrome (POTS).

I've endured all these health issues and tried to deal with and process intense trauma while simultaneously parenting four children and trying to not expose them to any of the trauma.

For everything that has happened in my life—all of the pain, all of the heartache, all of the times I wondered, *Why are these things happening to me?*—I can draw a direct line to something that happened in the TTI.

But I am survivor.

How do I know?

You can be a victim for 30 years, or you can be a victim for three seconds. But when you decide that you are not going to let your past experiences dictate your future, when you decide you are not going to let a period of your life keep you from opportunities, you are a survivor.

Life may make you anxious. You may struggle at work and at home. But if you never stop trying, regardless of your fears—that, to me, is the definition of a survivor.

And honestly, because we are dealing here with the buried memories of childhood trauma, survivor is a weird word. We're never actually done. We're never healed once and for all. That is why I prefer to call members of my community, *warriors*. Wherever you are on your journey, welcome.

Chapter One

STRICT PARENTS AND SNEAKY KIDS

Parenting is really hard. I actually find it ludicrous that when you have a baby and leave the hospital with this brand-new soul there isn't some kind of "parenting handbook" they give you. Without some kind of policies and procedures, we are likely to succumb to the pressure of how others around us parent or have the conditioning from our parents bubble to the surface.

Every day, we have to make a very conscious decision whether the way we parent is the way we *want* to parent our children. Every day presents a myriad of situations that require us to respond authentically in the moment.

Some nights, for example, when I put my kids to bed, they're scared. They cry and ask me to come back in the room and stay with them. I could say no. I could say, *You're old enough now not to worry about that.* Or I could engage them in a discussion.

"Why are you scared?" I choose to ask.

They might respond, "I'm scared of the dark."

"What about the dark scares you?" I ask them gently.

"I'm afraid someone is going to come and kidnap me."

I've noticed that is an innate fear many children share. And that greatest apprehension of a kid is what I was put through. That's what happened to me.

"That must be really scary to think about happening. I won't ever let that happen to you" I always respond.

At the age of 15, I was taken by two strangers in the middle of the night from my California home. I didn't know where I was going and I didn't know why. I was only told, "You are coming with me. We can do this the easy way or the hard way."

As soon as they announced that the hard way involved handcuffs, I chose the easy way to save myself the embarrassment and further trauma of flying on an airplane while cuffed. So I complied, which would become a repeating theme in my experiences over the next three and a half years.

Comply, never ask questions. Just, DO!

I didn't know these two individuals—a man and a woman. I never learned their names. I only knew that the man was huge. He was around six foot five inches and was called "Big John." I knew that because many other people at the lockdown treatment facility in Boise, Idaho, where I was deposited eight hours later had also been escorted there by Big John. The woman was petite but muscular.

I didn't have many interactions with them except for when they handed me a letter on the plane that was from my parents. That letter was basically about how much my parents loved me, but they were scared, and they thought this was the best thing for me. They wrote that they weren't abandoning me and that this didn't mean they didn't love me.

Bullshit, I thought. I was glad that the last thing I had said to them was, "I fucking hate you! And I'm never talking to you again!"

It was January 28th, 2001, when I arrived at the front doors of Intermountain Hospital after a long day of being kidnapped and scared. My first thought on hearing the magnetic doors that locked behind me was, *I've been abducted.*

I didn't know I would spend what seemed like an eternity there, six months in all, from January to July 2001. But I did know that I was never going to be the same again—and I wasn't. I could feel what was left of my childhood drain from me.

My feelings were so complex when I think back to them; I felt like a scared child again, yet I also knew I wouldn't ever be able to act like a child again. It was the same visceral reaction you have when you watch a natural disaster on TV wreaking havoc on its environment and inhabitants; that sinking feeling in your gut that tells you that nothing will ever be the same for them again. Only, I wasn't watching it on TV, I was in the natural disaster.

They took everything from me, my bags, my clothes. I wasn't allowed to have any of it because they had to find time to go through it all. And since it was Super Bowl weekend, the doctor wouldn't be in again until Tuesday. That meant I had to go three days without having any of my stuff.

Three days with no shoes, in the dead of winter in Boise where there was snow on the ground.

When I finally did get my shoes back, of course they had taken out the laces. I wasn't allowed to have anything that I could hurt myself with.

I couldn't have obvious things like razors, but I also couldn't even have a pencil because I could potentially use the eraser to rub my skin raw.

Before I reached Intermountain, self-harm was completely foreign to me. As I discovered later, you are always on "safety" when you first get to a psychiatric facility in case you harm yourself.

I was watched 24/7.

They said I could write a letter home, but I had to write it in crayon. I remember thinking, *How ironic* .... Yes, even at 15, I thought, *How ironic that this letter is written in crayon because I feel like such a child.*

19

I had spent the last two years thinking, *I know what I'm doing. I'm 14. I'm 15. My parents think I'm a baby. But I'm not.*

Then I got there and I'm writing letters home in crayon like a fucking baby.

I was so scared. It was that same feeling you get when you're four years old and you get lost in the mall. *What is going to happen now? Who's going to help me? There's no one. My life is over.* So I decided I better try apologizing for everything and appeal to my parents' better nature.

"Mom, Dad," I wrote, "Everyone here is crazy. You've made a mistake. You don't understand. This is not where I'm supposed to be. I'm so sorry. Please let me come home. If I come home, I promise I won't do anything else wrong. I'm really sorry for whatever I did."

Grounded

I had been acting out for a few years by that point. When I turned 13, my parents' grip on me started getting tighter and tighter. The tighter it got, the more uncomfortable and controlled I felt which caused me to push back and resist their rules.

I looked at my older brother, and he seemed to be having no issues, which made me feel like I belonged even less and so I rebelled more.

Strict parents make sneaky kids—that's what it comes down to. The more rules they had, the more I had to sneak around. That was a very normal way to parent at the time, but it didn't work for me, in part because I was autistic—(something we would only discover much later). The more I pushed against the rules or broke the rules, the more rules they had.

At the time, all I knew was that if it didn't make logical sense to me, I couldn't obey just for the sake of obeying.

"I can't date until I'm 16? Why?"

"You're too young."

"Okay, but why? Explain that to me."

The issue of pushing back on any rules set for me was compounded by my underlying need for independence and feeling like I didn't need anyone's help in the world, I was ready to leave the nest and fly! In reality, I was just supremely naive. In fact, I recall one conversation I had with my dad when I was about 11 when I called a family meeting:

"Dad, I want to talk about my living options"

"Your living options ... what do you mean?"

"I was thinking it would be best for me to get my own apartment."

"Oh? And how do you plan on paying for that?"

"Well, I thought you could pay for it ...."

A big point of contention came when I started to use the internet. We had a computer with AOL, and I found I was able to talk to people more easily on instant messenger than the kids at my school. I would connect with people my own age and then go meet them in person.

My parents had a huge problem with that (which is understandable) especially because everything in this digital world was so brand new. But their way of making sure I didn't break the rules was to use force. If they didn't want me on the internet past 10 p.m., they would simply lock up the modem in a cabinet with a chain.

However, since I have Ehlers-Danlos Syndrome (EDS) (which makes me very flexible) I could put my hand inside and re-plug the phone line into the back of the modem, then get my hand out again. They never knew because I would undo it when I was done. But one night, I forgot to unplug it again, and all hell broke loose.

Having four kids myself, I tried this kind of parenting out to see if it fit. I even tried spanking. It is what I experienced growing up, and I didn't know better.

So, for context, Jackson, or Jack as I call him, has the sweetest, most amazing heart of anyone I know. He is such a ball of love, empathy, and compassion. However, like me, he has anxiety, and sometimes when he is told "no" or "stop," he tends to push the limits to see how far he can go.

One of the weird things about anxiety is that it looks almost as like defiance. It isn't defiance, though; Jack is uncomfortable being anxious so he thinks, *I'm going to act in the opposite way to try to force my body into believing I'm not anxious and hopefully my brain will follow.*

I vividly remember one day driving on the highway when Jack was two-and-a-half years old and his sister, Harper, was a newborn. He kept repeatedly putting blankets over Harper's face in the car seat, posing what seemed to be a threat to her safety. I told him if he didn't stop that, I'd have to pull over and spank him. Well, he didn't stop, and I pulled over on the side of the road, pulled him out of his car seat, and explained why I had to spank him. Then, I spanked him. I was too scared of hurting him, so it wasn't very hard. I'll never forget what he did. He looked me dead in the eyes, smacked me right across the face and said, "No!"

I knew at that moment that physical punishment, which is how I was raised, would not work on my children, especially Jack. Instantly, I had an epiphany of how physical punishments only teach the child that it is okay to react to situations with aggression. "Alright, that's fair," I said to him calmly.

I never spanked any of my kids again. *But,* I remember thinking, *If I don't spank them, then what other methods should I use to get them to do what I know they should be doing?*

This train of thought took me back to my childhood again. *Control, I thought. How about I do what my parents did with me and control their lives so that the chances of mistakes happening are much lower, right?*

So I experimented with not creating space for them to make mistakes.

It backfired horribly.

I remember when the kids were young, the pediatrician would tell us to not let the kids have too much sugar and "junk food," so I tried to follow that as much as I could. I didn't buy sugar, for example.

I began to notice, though, that anytime my kids were around sugar, they would eat copious amounts of it. In fact, I noticed that any food that had any type of sugar in it was consumed at super high rates whenever they had the opportunity.

When Spencer and Jackson were 4 and 6 years old, I walked into their room to find 60 wrappers of various foods that they felt they had to hoard in their room and eat in private because they felt ashamed for liking and wanting to eat that food.

After hiring an expert, I learned I had created a hierarchy of foods and inadvertently made my kids feel shame for wanting certain foods. I also learned that by not having sweets available in the house, I was creating a scarcity for those foods. This is why when they were around them, they consumed so much. To them, they never knew when they'd get to see those kinds of food again.

So I immediately made tons of yummy foods and candy readily available.

Have they had cavities since? Absolutely! But if they aren't feeling shame and guilt, or dealing with an eating disorder, then a cavity is so worth it.

I've come to understand that when it comes to parenting, attempting to control your child's actions or outcomes may provide a sense of comfort to the parents, but in reality, it often has the opposite effect on the child. Instead of deterring them, it tends to increase their desire for the item or behavior you're trying to regulate.

Back when I was a young teenager and started to act out, my parents didn't teach me or allow me to make my own decisions. Instead, they read my diary and learned that I had started to smoke pot, so they took me for unannounced drug tests (where I peed in the cup and then tried to add some water to it as well). I started having sex and my mother's response was to track my periods.

I started struggling more in school, too. By the time I started ninth grade, I had been to a total of five schools, mostly small and intimate private schools, and I was relentlessly bullied in every single one of them. Most days ended with me crying on the way home from school.

I begged my parents to go to a big public high school. I think I wanted this because it gave me more options for friends and a better chance I'd find people to hang out with who wouldn't bully me. My parents complied and enrolled me in Newport Harbor High School, a big public school in Newport Beach, CA. With each passing day at that school, however, I got more lost and distracted by the number of kids, and my grades started to decline.

When nothing else seemed to produce the behavior they desired, my parents would simply ground me. I'd rebel, and then they'd ground me some more.

It got to the point, just before I was sent away, where I was grounded for months and months continually.

When you're looking at, say, six months of being grounded... you're so deep in a hole, you think, *I might as well just go for it—* whatever the illicit behavior happens to be.

Here's a poem that I wrote that expresses the way that vicious cycle felt to a 15-year-old.

Grounded, within the
Boundaries of those who
Love you, you feel betrayal.
Grounded, feeling the
Hatred bind between
Your blood, your skin.
Family, in your heart,
You need them, you
Love them, you can't live
Without, but in your
Soul, fuck them, you
Don't need them.

One day my best friend Stacy and I decided we wanted to skip school. There was nothing holding me back since I was already on an extended period of being grounded anyway.

We walked around for a little bit and then went to the 7-Eleven. A man who looked homeless was sitting out front and was on a bike. We didn't know what to make of him, so we said, "Hey, will you buy us some beer?"

His response was, "Sure, if you buy me a bagel."

That seemed like a reasonable trade-off at the time.

The man, who said his name was Len and that he was 32, smiled, stood up, and walked inside as Stacy and I scurried around the corner, giggling, to hide.

Len gave us the beer, and then he started following us. We were walking through the heart of Costa Mesa, which has some rough parts of town, so for a while, we didn't mind having him follow us as it made us feel less scared; he was an adult, after all. However, once we started to roam through the alleys, we still didn't understand why he wouldn't leave us alone.

At one point, we entered an alley, and he pulled up right in front of us on his bike, blocking our way. He pulled out a knife that he had, but almost in a non-threatening way.

"Isn't this cool?" he asked us.

By this point, I was feeling extremely drunk and eventually blacked out.

When I came to, we were in a park adjacent to the alley, and my pants were around my ankles. I looked up and saw Stacy basically straddling Len. She was completely unconscious and slumped over his left shoulder while he kissed her neck.

My heart started to pound in fear. I yelled, "Stacy! Stacy!" Then I pulled up my pants and could hear someone walking down one of the park paths.

I pulled Stacy off Len and shook her to try to wake her up, as Len ran away.

The person walking down the path was actually a police officer. He stopped me and asked, "Aren't you supposed to be in school?"

"No, we're in a home period," I responded. (This was a lie.)

We didn't tell him anything about what had just happened, even though we knew Len had sexually assaulted us. We were so scared of getting in trouble. I thought I was being clever when the policeman asked for my address, and I gave him my exact address only with the wrong zip code.

There is really no way the police officer could not have seen at least some of the inappropriate things that had just taken place. If I saw a grown man with two girls in a park during school hours and my mere presence caused the man to run, I'd like to think I would have made the decision to utilize my time by catching the man rather than interrogating "truant" girls.

I do realize, however, that this was in the year 2000, and things were much different back then. Sexual assaults were not treated seriously yet, and many times if a young person was seen with an older person, the blame was put on the younger person for being a tease or temptress instead of the older person being seen as the sexual predator they were.

On the walk back to school, we debated as to whether we should tell anyone about the events of the day. We decided that we would only tell people what had happened if we got caught for leaving campus, otherwise we would keep it a secret. However, because we were petrified of getting in trouble for leaving campus and drinking, we decided that in the event we got caught, we would tell them everything that had happened with Len—but we'd lie and say he abducted us from campus (with the knife that we knew he had) and then forced us to drink.

It's interesting now that we tried to portray ourselves as victims of an abduction when three weeks later, I would actually be abducted myself.

We ended up getting caught for being absent from school, and we told the planned lie. Now the police were involved again, but they immediately handed it over to some detectives from the FBI. They brought Stacy and me to a special victim's unit, where we were interviewed by a psychologist, and they separated us so we couldn't talk to each other. I was behind a double-paned window that looked like glass, but you couldn't see through it. I knew there were people on the other side watching our entire interaction.

The psychologist pulled out these stuffed animals and said, "Why don't you show me with these bears what he did to you?" She made me put the bears in different positions. Everything was true about the story I told except for the parts where he forced us to leave campus and forced us to drink. He had pulled a knife on us, and he had sexually assaulted us. They even collected our underwear to test forensically; they were taking everything very seriously.

Later that week, I got called to the principal's office over the loudspeaker at school. I didn't think anything of it at first because the whole investigation was being conducted off school grounds, but as I went in, I saw Stacy walking out. She whispered, "I'm sorry," and I knew she had told the truth.

A detective from the FBI was in the office. He told me, "Stacy came forward with the truth." They were so angry with me, and I was crying.

I pled with him, "I'm so sorry, but the other stuff was true. I just didn't want to get in trouble."

He said, "Why would we believe you now? You're obviously lying."

I came to find out that they had found Len, who was living in a motel. They even found the exact knife I described, but all of the charges were dropped because we had drunk willingly and we had lied about how we had left campus. We were labeled and stigmatized.

We were officially "troubled teens."

As I have spoken to survivors in this community throughout the years, it's become clear that a prior sexual assault or rape before entering the Troubled Teen Industry seems to be extremely prevalent. In fact, I would venture to say that a vast majority of teens entering the industry have a prior trauma history.

Because we lied, the school expelled both of us, citing the zero-tolerance policy that had been newly installed within the school systems. Basically, that law stated that if you consume alcohol or drugs during school hours, you don't get a second strike. It didn't even matter that I hadn't consumed alcohol at the school itself. I was allowed to finish that semester in detention, which meant I went to school in a trailer on campus for the few weeks I had left. Then they kicked me out, unapologetically. At which point, my parents must have thought, *Fuck, what do we do now?*

Chapter Two

HOW AM I
SUPPOSED TO BELONG?

If you were to talk to 15-year-old me about my choices during that period, I would probably say some version of, "This is what everyone is doing …." Maybe I would even tell you the whole truth—that I had no idea who I was and I wanted friends.

Being an undiagnosed autistic, it was hard for me to make friends. I didn't see it at the time, but I very much think I was viewed as socially off. People could just "tell" that I was different. I struggled to catch social cues of people not wanting to talk to me anymore or changing the subject during conversations which made it hard to detect when others wanted to change the subject or end the conversation. I often interrupted people because I did not understand the conversational dynamics. I also emoted every single thing I felt and had no filter whatsoever (this was definitely connected to my ADHD as well).

Drinking and smoking pot was how I became accepted, by hanging out with the counterculture kids who were open to anyone. It also made me feel "better" when I smoked pot. Looking back, I think that I enjoyed smoking pot because it made me feel less affected by my knowledge that I didn't fit in. I was willing to do anything to fit in.

Even in my journal I was lying. I would personify myself as someone who I wasn't, talk about doing drugs that I had never done and what it was like. It was almost like I was trying to create a life for myself; however this made my parents think everything was much worse than it actually was.

Why did I want so badly to pretend I was someone else? I can't remember a defining moment of when I became aware of the fact I was adopted, it always seemed to be something I was aware of because my parents were always honest with me. Being adopted, however, always made me feel like I didn't fit in with my family. While self imposed, that feeling was heightened when I entered high school and didn't fit in there, either. All in all, it was a period of time when I was just really confused and desperately wanted to fit in. But how do you fit in within your family, let alone the world, if you don't know who you are yet?

To understand why I felt like a misfit, you have to understand my family dynamics.

My father was the CEO of a Fortune 500 company. He and my mother both graduated from Northwestern University. My father went to Harvard Business School, while my mother supported them as a High School biology teacher.

My brother, Grant, built his first computer by around age 11, started his first business in high school and graduated with a 4.3 GPA. Then he graduated from Northwestern University and went on to found a company, Vodori, that now has 35-plus employees in Chicago.

There was never pressure from my parents to be like Grant; having Grant as a brother made me put that pressure on myself.

Why can't I get good grades as easily as Grant? I would ask myself.
Why can't I get into good colleges like Grant?
Why can't I have it easy like Grant?

It is interesting to look back at this narrative I created surrounding my brother because Grant was actually struggling internally, it just wasn't showing outwardly. While I was learning to mask my autism, Grant was learning to mask his sexuality.

Grant came out as being gay at age 26, and during this time that I had personified him as this person without any problems, he admits he was indeed in great distress and suffering inside from hiding who he was. Coincidently, this likely contributed to his desire to succeed in the other outward-facing areas of his life that others could see. It allowed him to focus his energy elsewhere to ignore dealing with his sexuality.

Don't get me wrong, I actually think my parents were very good parents for an adopted child. They would be good parents for any child. This was a self-imposed feeling.

How was I supposed to belong in this family?

I felt like the fuck-up long before I was labeled a fuck-up and a troubled teen. All that really did was solidify that I was a problem, and all I brought was heartache. I already had that in my brain. Everything that followed was just a self-fulfilling prophecy.

While I may have had my doubts about whether or not I belonged in my family, I was certain I didn't belong in the psychiatric hospital.

I had never been around kids with diagnoses like schizophrenia and bipolar disorder. I had never had a roommate talk to her deceased boyfriend in the middle of the night, or seen someone eat cigarette butts, or watched someone use a razor to slit their wrists while I had to yell "Safety issue!" out of my door.

What is the worst someone could say about me? That I was a bad daughter? And yet, I ended up in the psych hospital, so maybe something was going on that I didn't see.

If I was bad enough to get rid of, then maybe I was missing something.

Almost daily, one of the other patients would have to get restrained. For whatever reason, they would just lose it and start screaming. Then you would hear a code being called over the intercom, and all of the muscular staff from the other units would come running with all the keys on their belt jangling.

There might be four or five of them; they'd throw the kid down on the ground face-first and have a couple of staff hold his arms while another staff member put his knee in between the kid's shoulder blades.

If that didn't stop the ruckus, another staff member would pull down the kid's pants and stick a long needle filled with some kind of tranquilizer into his or her rear end. We colloquially referred to that injection as "booty juice."

Once the booty juice was administered, you would see the kids go limp, and they would be carried into the Quiet Room behind the nurse's station. The "QR," as it was called, was a padded room with a shatterproof 8x10 glass window on the door. There was a bed in the middle with what looked like almost medieval leather bindings to strap somebody in. The room also had a lock on the outside of the door so the kids would have to stay there until they were calm.

I remember anxiously watching the QR window hours after a restraint, waiting to see a child's face pop up into view to make sure they survived it. You would randomly see a kid's head pop up, and they'd look very tired and drugged. Well, they *were* drugged. They would lightly tap the window until a nurse noticed and asked, "Are you going to be good now?"

I watched these people getting restrained, and to me, it looked like they were being cared for.

I didn't feel like I was getting any positive attention in the hospital.

I was desperate for love.

So one day, I thought, *Maybe I should do that.*

Now, I'm not that kind of person. I'm not out of control; I've never been like that. Even when I get attitude, I'm not aggressive; I've never been threatening in my entire life. Nonetheless, I decided I'd try to act in a way that would get me restrained.

I started screaming at the staff and throwing stuff, yelling, "Ah! I'm so mad!" And they just looked up, and they said, "Knock it off, Mary." (Mary was the name I went by in the hospital, for reasons I explained earlier.)

I tried so hard, and they just looked at me like, "Yeah, we don't believe you."

While this is obviously a funny story to those who know me, it is also very sad. In essence, it highlights exactly what happens to families when children do not receive the needed amount of love, affection, and support; they turn to negative behaviors to see if that works. I only tried that once before realizing it wouldn't work.

Then I gave up on trying to get any attention at all.

Thirty-Six Thinking Errors

The hospital was extremely strict. For each 15-minute segment of the day, the staff would rate your behavior during that time with a score of 0–10. The score was given in increments of 2 on what we called a "tracking sheet." They had to make it complicated, though. A "good" or "standard" day was getting all 6's, but if you get a 0, 2, or 4, they cost against you, and the way they calculated that was by assigning money to each number, as follows:

0—Costs you 75 cents

2—Costs you 50 cents

4—Costs you 25 cents

The current level you are on dictates how much "money" you can lose each day without losing your level or going on level freeze.

Usually, Level 0's were able to have one dollar on their tracking sheet, but as you moved up the levels, you were allowed to have less money.

Confused yet?

It was not a game designed for the patient to win.

For instance, if you were on level 2, you might only be able to get 50 cents, which means if you were anything but amazing for 30 minutes in the day, you could lose your level. Even if you were in something like group therapy that's an hour long and you forgot to bring your tracking sheet, you would likely be on level freeze.

It was insanity.

They wanted you to feel completely out of control in your daily life.

There were motion sensors in the middle of every patient's room. If you went to the bathroom in the middle of the night, an alarm goes off in the nurse's station, indicating danger because they're trying to protect the patients from hurting each other. And they did bed checks every 30 minutes—so even if you are trying to sleep—there is always someone coming in to make sure you're still in your bed.

I don't know if I ever got a full night's sleep the entire time I was there.

They invented a special kind of hell for me, called "Random Draw." That meant if there was any kind of programming, whether it was art therapy, anger management, going outside, going to PE, or watching a movie, I had to draw from one of those orange bio-hazard bags.

Inside the bag were ten folded pieces of paper. My doctor determined how many of those ten pieces of paper said "yes" and how many said "no," based on how he thought I was doing at the time. I started off with nine no's and one yes, which meant I almost never got to go to the cafeteria for lunch, or whatever the rest of the group was doing.

If I got a no, which I almost always did, I was assigned to *Desk Space*. That meant I had to sit at my desk and write, and write, and write. They gave me a list of the "Thirty-Six Thinking Errors," and I had to write two pages about each one and how they applied to my life.

"Lying by Omission."

"Self-Justification."

"The Victim Stance."

Some of these things were self-explanatory. But how was I supposed to write two pages on "Sentimentality" with this as the cue:

"Sentimentality: I am often excessively sentimental about my mother, old people, invalids, animals, babies, my love attachments, plans for the future, and so on. Criminal sentimentality is inconsistent and does not deter criminal thinking and actions."

Everything was criminal.

"Fragmentation: This is a very basic feature of my criminal personality."

"Pride: Criminal pride preserves my rigid self-image as a powerful, totally self-determining person."

But I wasn't a criminal. So in order to give them what they wanted, I had to lie. I had already been labeled as an addict so if I didn't tell the story of an addict, then I was being manipulative, sneaky, and dishonest. I had to change my actual life story to accommodate their opinion.

In my journal from those days, you can read, "In the past, drugs and alcohol have played a major role in my life, like I needed to smoke to get through the day."

(I never once had to smoke to get through the day.)

"I think this choice affected my family greatly. For my drug history, I am just going to say what drugs I have done and how many times."

But when you read my total drug history, it says: "I drank 10 times. I have done acid one time."

(I actually realized later that it was not acid. It was fake and probably worked via the placebo effect.)

"I have snorted speed once. I have smoked weed, but don't know how many times."

Just as I had to lie and pretend to be an addict, I had to lie about having anger issues. (I don't.)

I had to lie and pretend to have depression. (I don't.)

Then they said I had oppositional defiant disorder (ODD).

Okay, so let's get this straight: You take a teenager—all of whom likely have ODD on some level—and you kidnap them in the middle of the night. You put them around other kids who obviously have very high support needs. Then you tell them that they need to change the fact that they always push back against authority and have a high need for control.

Of course, I wanted control! I was grasping to be able to control anything in my life.

My whole life was spinning out of control.

But because ODD doesn't really have a standard medication, which they loved to dole out regularly, I was also diagnosed with bipolar disorder, type II. I was put on antipsychotics, mood stabilizers, and tranquilizers.

Because of how powerful the medications were, I had head-aches every day. They made me throw up. They made me groggy. I dreaded the midday meds because it felt like I was fighting a sleeping pill during what they considered "school."

In my journals, you can read, "I'm so tired. I feel so sick. They're going to get mad at me because I feel like I want to fall asleep ...." and then you'll see my handwriting change and trail off the page as the dizziness set in. It's just so sad.

At night we would get our medications from the nurse's station. After showing them our mouths to ensure we hadn't "cheeked" the meds, we had to sit in the community room for a while so they could make sure no one had an immediate adverse reaction.

Once we were allowed to go back to our room, it was like a race against the clock to get to bed. I have vivid memories of walking along the right side of the hallway, running my fingertips over the textured bumps of that wall as it held me up, trying to get back to my room before I fell over from the dizziness.

They made me read Danielle Steel's book, *His Bright Light*, about her son who had bipolar disorder. It turned out to be one of my favorite books, actually. They wanted me to understand what having bipolar type II was like, only I didn't have it. They had falsely categorized my behaviors into those buckets.

They said, "When you're using and smoking, you're manic. The reason why you want to sleep in every morning, and don't want to get up, is because you're in a depressive state ...."

But I never knew what depression was until I started taking their medication, which *made* me depressed. It wasn't until I suffered postpartum depression many years later that I ever knew what genuine depression felt like.

I must have been having a Pink Floyd moment of clarity when I scrawled in my journal, "We don't need no medication, nurses leave us kids alone." But I also understood something more when I wrote, "It's all about the money!"

At the time, I was clueless as to the profit-driven industry that existed, but I could still feel how they all wanted us all to be the same.

Even at that young age, I thought it was strange that almost everyone had bipolar disorder. No one knew they had bipolar disorder before, but now all of a sudden, we're on the same kind of medication? How is that possible?

Because they wanted us to have diagnosis codes that yielded longer stays.

They wanted us to have more significant problems than we actually had, to justify keeping us there longer and receiving more money.

My doctor didn't like that I pushed back on this. He wrote a long letter to my parents in which he said the following (I have not edited his words):

"Specifically with your daughter, at this point, she has some naiveté in that she is still focusing upon 'I am fine, you are wrong in terms of classifying me as bipolar.' She also is still at that stage where to her, normal is what she was, and she hasn't been under sufficient control long for enough to be able to recognize what truly being normal is."

This letter, from Dr. Heyrend, MD of Boise Idaho, seems like it is out of the Victorian era, but it is from *this century*. He went on to say:

"This, I hope, you will understand that I feel one of the dangers that your daughter has is that when she is in a manic state and if she is on the run and not under your direct supervision, what is going to happen is that there is a high, high potential risk of her being involved in sexual behaviors with a high likelihood of very painful consequences.

"I might add that one of the factors that we have discovered in our histories of adolescent bipolar females is the frequency in which either the father or the mother was bipolar, and there is a loss of control in out-of-wedlock teen pregnancies …. The fact that bipolar females are more sexually reactive has been well-known for centuries."

Sufficient Control for Long Enough

From where I sit now, I see that my precociousness, what they labeled as defiance, was really my strength. I think true character begins that way when you are a young teenager. I see it in my daughter, Spencer. What is seen as being "hard to handle" is, to my mind, a prediction that she will one day turn into the strongest woman you'll ever know. Does she need some guidance? Sure, along with patience and love while we wait for her brain and her heart to negotiate how that strength is going to play out. But it always starts with defiance, with pushing back, with not taking things at face value. That, in itself, is representative of intelligence and the complex thinking involved in learning to think for yourself. I never want her to lose that.

If we are going to diagnose teenagers, can we at least put a "situational" in front of whatever label we seek to apply?

Situational depression.

Situational anxiety.

When someone is in a situation where they are being held against their will, and they are scared, and feeling hopeless, can we say they have *situational* oppositional defiant disorder? Can we give them a safe space, a conversation, and see if that changes things?

That is not what happened to me. Instead, I was made to feel like I could do nothing to help myself.

No one was there for me, so I might as well just give up and commit to the program. That's how they get you to move forward.

Martin Seligman coined the term "learned helplessness" to describe a situation where punishment is inescapable. In one of his experiments in the late sixties, when rats received inescapable shocks, they would no longer try to escape (as opposed to if the shocks were escapable). They had reached a place where they didn't care what happened to them. If pushing a button meant a shock they would just do it anyway because they could no longer either fight or flee.

I was pushed into that place of, *I can't run. I can't hide. I can't win this battle. So I'm going to sit here and let it destroy me.*

You can see evidence of this in my relationship with food in the hospital. I gained sixty pounds in the six months I was there. For one thing, what they served in the hospital was dreadful, with astronomically high caloric content. I was also heavily medicated, and my medications all had the side effect of weight gain. In addition to that, we had a continuous lack of good exercise.

Even more relevant than those factors, was that food had become a coping mechanism. Even if the food was terrible, I would want seconds and thirds because it helped me feel better about what was going on.

I remember being so excited for food, all the time. There was nothing else for comfort. Seeing as I was unmedicated for my ADHD during this time (due to their certainty that I was bipolar instead), my dopamine needs weren't being met; hence the binge eating.

Food was the one thing I could control.

When my parents came to visit, the hospital would give us a pass to leave the premises. This pass, though, was often held over your head as leverage to receive compliance. They would constantly tell you that if your tracking sheet didn't look good the day of your pass, they would take your visit with your family away. Everything was designed to have you believe that the quality of your existence depended on how you were viewed from the outside.

I remember my mother taking me to the mall because I had gained so much weight that I needed all new clothes. This was the time that everyone was into Hot Topic and wearing the JNCO jeans they sold there. The jeans I bought were five sizes larger than I had ever needed in the past.

I wrote in my journal that day after having to try on clothes at the store, "It really upset me what happened. Today, I'm wearing really baggy clothes and lots of makeup …."

But it didn't inspire me to change anything. Eating and enjoying food was the highlight of my day. It was the one piece of the day that created joy.

I was not alone. I saw many people go into these facilities that didn't have any behaviors that could be considered disordered eating but they came out with them. Some people learned how to vomit after meals. I learned how to binge eat my feelings.

Out of the Frying Pan

When I first got to the hospital, I didn't know how long I was going to be there. I think it was at least a month before I was even given my treatment plan, which consisted of various ways that I needed to change myself like giving up control, not talking back, being honest, and completing numerous writing assignments.

Being the methodological person I am, I began checking off the list on my treatment plan. As I completed each prescribed action, I could see that I was moving incrementally closer to completion. But then—just when it looked like I was almost done—a new treatment plan would arise, effectively moving the goalpost. this happened many times.

I wouldn't be surprised if some of the reason they held on to me so long was for financial gain. That would explain why everything seemed so delayed, and why there were so many setbacks based on small things like not listening or respecting authority.

Let's say I actually was bipolar. There's no reason a child with bipolar disorder should be in a mental institution for six months. If I needed to be stabilized on certain medications that would be a short stay. Even if I was experiencing psychosis, that's still not guaranteed to be a six-month stay.

Finally, my therapist started to tell me about this magical place called "Chrysalis," where I was to go for the remainder of high school. They had all this acreage there and lots of animals. They even had horses!

They made this place seem like a utopia, and I can read in my journal how hard I tried to maintain a certain level of staff approval so that I would be able to be let out.

I didn't know at the time that I was jumping out of the frying pan and into the fire.

Chapter Three

THEY'RE NOT TROUBLED, THEY'RE JUST TEENS

The Troubled Teen Industry (TTI) has gone through many phases, but at its root there are two concepts. The first, as the name would indicate, is the existence of the "troubled teen" and the second is "tough love."

Let's take tough love first. Some of the early marketing literally shows a kid with their arms crossed and the caption: "Troubled teen? We can fix that." This initially appealed to parents from the baby boomer generation, who had in turn been parented by individuals coming of age during the Great Depression or World War II, the so-called Greatest Generation.

The essence of a tough love approach to parenting was: Break the rules and you will be punished. You'll get whipped with a belt or a wooden spoon or you'll get grounded for years or you'll be sent to military school.

The basis of tough love was the notion that children don't learn unless they simultaneously suffer, either physically or emotionally. If you don't control your kids, they won't turn out to be productive members of society. If you don't show them what it means to have pain, they'll cause other people pain.

This approach is different from saying that there need to be natural consequences. If a kid is refusing to go to school, for example, it isn't tough love for them to not get their diploma. That's a natural consequence. Rather, tough love, in both its inception and its execution, implies that a child has to go through something alone, without support.

Continuing with the school refusal example, tough love may look like kicking the kid out of the family home for dropping out of school, telling them, "If you are under our roof, you follow our rules. If you don't follow the rules, you don't have a home." It is instilling more pain than the situation would normally cause to somehow "help them learn" to not do it again.

That is something I will never agree with.

Love shouldn't hurt.

It can be hard in a moment of anger to feel love for a kid who is acting out. At the end of the day, though, love is not only an emotion. To me, love is a decision, every single day, to wake up and be there for a person, unconditionally. That goes for anyone—children, spouse, parents, other family members or friends.

We need to change the way we think about our children's ups and downs of adolescence. If we have the habit of thinking of our children as "behaving badly," that will automatically put us into a "punishment" mentality as a result. We will naturally think, "Well, if they are going to behave badly, then there will be consequences."

What if we instead thought of our children as "struggling" to handle difficult situations or feelings? Viewing things in this way will allow parents to naturally feel encouraged to help them through these times, rather than enticed to punish them.

That was not my experience in the TTI. Instead, you can read in my journal, "I wake up every morning feeling like crap and go to bed feeling like crap. In the day, I feel like crap. And also get crap for all the crap I give all of the people for their crap." That was the effect of the relentless negativity of a tough love approach that was designed to create a rock bottom so that a kid would conform.

To further examine the Troubled Teen Industry, let's look at that catch-all phrase, "troubled teens."

First of all, a majority of these "troubled teens" are just normal teens. There *are* genuinely troubled teens, but they do not make up the vast majority. A genuinely troubled teen, in my mind, is someone who absolutely requires supervision around the clock because they might be a danger to themselves or others. For example, someone who might be experiencing active suicidal ideation or sociopathic urges is a teen that is experiencing genuine trouble and may require outside monitoring.

There's a big difference between a teen who is struggling educationally, with mental health, or with learning disabilities versus a genuinely troubled teen. And yet, as I mentioned previously about what happens if we don't put "situational" before a diagnosis and then that diagnosis sticks for life, applying the adjective "troubled" to a kid stays with them forever too.

Even if society at large has forgotten about my adolescent years, the label of "troubled teen" is forever ingrained in my brain. I am troubled. And because I am troubled, I am never good enough.

In my work with parents of struggling teens who are desperately searching for answers, I have noticed a general trend of parents unknowingly pathologizing adolescence. Instead of trying to understand the underlying causes of the behaviors they feel are worthy of being sent away for, such as mental health struggles or educational difficulties, they label them as "troubled." The most common behaviors in this category are having sex, exploring their gender or sexual identity, sneaking out of the house, substance use, pushing back on authority, and skipping school.

Any, all or some of those behaviors are on my long list of potential behaviors that teens may exhibit that are still part of normal development as they mature.

It is also very normal for parents to be scared. This is where the TTI sees its prey and swoops in for the kill. The TTI thrives on manipulation, and deceptive marketing, fear tactics, and the pathologizing of normal adolescent behavior. These are its weapons of choice. They scare parents into thinking that their child will not be successful in life unless they make some rather drastic decisions.

What makes this so appalling to me is the way it completely negates the research showing that, in most cases of at-risk behavior in adolescence, simply being there and loving them through it while allowing them to be a part of the household is the best way to ensure a good end result. Research also shows that the majority of teens that are doing drugs will not become addicts; a majority of teens having sex are not going to become prostitutes.

There is a natural trajectory through the teenage years, and short of the extreme crises that I mentioned requiring intervention, we don't need to intervene in a substantially abusive way, like sending them to an outside institution. They will figure life out.

In my case, some of my acting out came from being a normal teenager. Some of it came from being adopted and the trauma associated with not feeling like I fit in. That is actually closely tied in with being a teenager because it makes the high-level drive of fitting in as a teenager harder; there was also the tendency to not listen to my parents as much because they were my adopted parents. Finally, some of my challenges came from being autistic. Yet none of these reasons should ever warrant institutionalization.

To better understand childhood development I want to illuminate Erik Erikson's work where he identified eight key stages of normal psychosocial development. These stages involve dealing with significant conflicts that shape an individual's personality as they mature. Things like learning trust versus mistrust and autonomy versus shame.

In the fifth stage, identity versus role confusion (ages 12–18), adolescents strive to establish their personal identities while facing challenges like social interactions and moral dilemmas. Recognizable signs of youth being in this stage include withdrawing from responsibilities, testing boundaries, defiance, rebellion, reluctance to complete tasks, and power struggles with adults. This highlights the challenges adolescents encounter as they navigate this critical phase of development.

Let that soak in for a second and think back to the main reasons kids are being sent into this industry. They are eerily similar.

In essence, so many of the behaviors that currently warrant youth being sent away are behaviors that are to be expected in the normal course of adolescent development. It is the role of parents during this somewhat unpleasant time to focus on supporting their children the best they can, not controlling or fixing them. Children rely on the consistency of a parent or caregiver attending to their needs. That is what forms attachment—an adult responding to their needs and bids for attention.

Attachment Theory, first developed by psychologists John Bowlby and Mary Ainsworth, teaches the difference between secure attachment and anxious attachment. One of the crucial factors that creates a secure attachment with a caregiver is that they are always responding in a consistent way to a child's needs. However, attachment is never formed through control.

What are we doing when we send kids away to facilities? We know that their needs aren't being met, because upon leaving many refer to themselves as survivors. Even the caregivers at the facilities know that graduates refer to themselves as survivors. How are these kids going to form an attachment with their parents now? Instead of healthy attachment, kids leave these facilities believing their needs are not going to be met by their parents. But, even more importantly, kids believe their needs aren't going to be met by anyone, so they cease to ask for any help.

The Teenage Years are Scary for Parents

I understand that the teenage years are scary for parents. My oldest daughter, Spencer, is almost 13 and is a mini-me. She is spicy. Spencer is starting down the road of a lot of the behaviors that my parents got so frustrated with me for and I struggle with how to raise a child who is entering that fifth stage that I was in when I got sent away. At this point in my life, I am right in the thick of it, where I can feel that karma coming for me. I know what it's like to be fed up and to think, *How the hell do we fix this?* I know what it's like to feel like there are no answers, so I'm not just a survivor speaking out; I'm also a parent of a teen.

I can empathize with what is going on inside a parent's head when they're considering a TTI. They're desperate. They're scared their child is going to die and they are trying to find experts and options. Community-based resources exist but they can be expensive and a lot of them aren't covered by a family's insurance plan. In addition to that, they are harder to find. If you're a single mom, for example, you may not have that time. Even if there are two parents at home, do either or both of them have the humility to recognize that their struggling teen's issue is, in fact, a family issue?

Recently, our family entered a tough phase for both Spencer, an established adolescent, and Jackson, who is beginning to enter that hard stage. Gone are the days (like when they were toddlers) of Ben and I being able to simply redirect their negative behaviors. Instead, we have had to say hello to the days of being called the worst parents in the world, getting told they hated us, and watching them lose motivation in school. They're also pushing back on rules and boundaries and dishing out the kind of intense gaslighting you'd expect out of a grown-ass person when you try to talk to them about something. If it weren't so troublesome, I would be impressed at the sheer intellect they are demonstrating!

Ben and I were at our wit's end. This marks the point where most parents cave. When it seems too much to handle, they seek a professional's help.

We did need a professional's help, but not for the kids—for us.

Instead of hiring an educational consultant to find a place to send them where they can "learn their lesson," we hired a parent coach to teach us how we can become better parents for our children.

How is it that the burden falls on the children themselves when behaviors, viewed as troublesome, are exhibited? They are children. Children have immature prefrontal cortexes that make it nearly impossible to master things like planning, prioritizing, and making good decisions. It is up to us parents, and our fully developed prefrontal cortexes, to make the necessary changes to meet the child where they are at.

Even in my own parenting journey, I've noticed a tendency to instinctively, albeit erroneously, think about my own children as something I "own"—a byproduct of me. I mean, I did make them right? I think it happens because, for so many years after birth, their survival was literally dependent on me, and viewing them as extensions of us keeps them alive. But they are individuals, regardless of whether they're 15 or 32, and they should be part of the discussion if it involves their life. They should have a say in what is happening to them.

We found the parent coach on TikTok, of all places, and it took about two weeks of sessions with them to gain parenting tools that were already helping! The beauty in this approach is that Spencer and Jackson had no idea we even hired someone, and they were free from any stigma of being "troubled," or having "something wrong with them they need to fix."

A parent coach is one of many solutions that could work in these scenarios, so long as that solution involves the whole family, and not just the child. It's imperative the kids don't view themselves as the problem because there is nothing wrong with them.

However, our kids definitely thought there was something wrong with us when we changed our parenting tactics overnight, started talking about feelings all the time, and engaged in what we called "heart talks" when there was conflict between family members. I would venture to guess they likely assume we joined a cult of some sort, but I'll take that over them assuming they are "bad" or "unloved" any day.

Do we as parents have the bandwidth for all of this, though, when we are actively freaking out? Or are we likely to pull the trigger on an option that seems all-encompassing, immediate, and easy to execute? Other options almost don't stand a chance when you are pitched a "solution" that is phrased as being the only option to save your child's life. When you take into account that fearmongering is often utilized, then parents who send their kids away aren't even really making a choice. They are just trying to help keep their kid from dying and haven't been given any other options.

I know that my parents made the best decision they could with the information they had back then. They were told by multiple "professionals" that the TTI was the only answer for me. They were very much given a life-or-death decision, or so they thought, and they tried to make the right call.

I'm not trying to excuse everything my parents did. For instance, I would have liked more dialogue around some of the touchy subjects such as sex and dating in my adolescence.

When I read my diary from before I got sent away, I noticed that my boyfriends were 100 percent taking advantage of me. I wrote about how they wanted to go on the webcam and perform sexual acts and I didn't want to, because I felt uncomfortable.

The verbal abuse that I accepted from these guys alone should have been a red flag, and if my parents read my diary I could certainly have benefitted from a conversation about the way guys should be treating you, and what "healthy" relationships should look like. I am definitely going to have those sex positive conversations with my children.

My personal parenting belief is that the more experiences my child can have under my roof, the more I can teach them. I'd rather they have their earliest dating years occur under my supervision, so I can help them understand the different stages and situations that arise in relationships.

I know my parents' motives were not suspect. Growing up, my mom was always my biggest advocate from a mental health standpoint. Before I was diagnosed with ADHD in grade school, I was misunderstood by almost all my teachers. They viewed me as disruptive and rude until my mom brought in a world-renowned ADHD specialist to educate them. They assumed I was being this way intentionally because I couldn't understand the material being taught. This was before ADHD was known by most people, and it certainly wasn't understood by teachers. One teacher actually apologized to my mom after, and said, "You're right. She actually is very intelligent. She just can't sit still or focus."

My mother also found me a neuropsychologist, a therapist, and different support groups. She didn't just fly blind. She went off the recommendations of the experts with whom she was constantly consulting. So it made sense that by the time I got to high school, she would do the same thing.

When the educational consultant they were using, the neuropsychologist and the neuropsychiatrist all agreed, well then, my parents went with their recommendations.

At Chrysalis, I would meet girls—"sisters," as we were told to call each other—and we would compare notes. My parents definitely fell into the category of parents who thought they were doing the right thing. They were trying their best to help their kid get better.

However, those weren't the only kinds of parents I heard about. I heard about the parents who just didn't want to parent anymore and were looking for the easy way out. Maybe these parents—and they still exist today—were tired. They'd had it.

Maybe they wanted to get a divorce or start a new relationship away from the prying eyes of a difficult teenager.

Maybe they themselves had been raised very conservatively in terms of politics, culture and/or religion, and they didn't want to communicate with their children.

Maybe they didn't want to be vulnerable; they would rather have all of the issues hidden. They had the mentality of see no evil, hear no evil, speak no evil. If your kid is doing something bad, you hide your kid. You send them away to be fixed and then they can come back.

There were also parents who subscribed to the tough love beliefs mentioned earlier. These parents might have experienced some kind of child abuse themselves, yet think they turned out fine—successful even—and it's because of what they had to go through. They may believe that because of their own experiences, their children need to be treated very roughly in order to turn out okay too. This was probably the least common type of parent I saw in Chrysalis, but they do exist. Those are the adults who may be fully aware of some of the things that go on in the TTI yet turn a blind eye to it.

What any parent willing to make the decision to send their child away to these facilities may not understand, though, is what that really entails. It is one thing to be desperate to find help for your child, but at what lengths will a parent go to make that happen? Will they sign away their rights to their child?

Most of these programs go so far as to make parents sign away their guardianship to ensure they have full power and control over the kids.

Think about that for a second.

Would you do it?

Later in life, these parents may not have a relationship with their children, and they will have to own the fact that they made a gigantic mistake. A mistake that they may find they can never rectify in regard to the hurt they caused their children. Those are things that no parent should have to go through. It emphasizes the reality that survivors are not the only victims here; many of the parents are victims as well.

Blame Where Blame is Due

The list of victims doesn't stop with the survivors and their parents. We also have school districts that utilize taxpayer dollars to send children to facilities through their Individualized Education Plan (IEP) They assume these programs are safe because they are approved by the Department of Education.

We also have disability rights organizations, attorneys, foster systems, medical and mental health professionals, and juvenile justice advocates who facilitate the placement of youth in these facilities—none of these people have an accurate idea of what goes on behind closed doors.

For the most part, these entities have a youth's best interest at heart and are trying to help. But they are operating on misinformation that has either been miscommunicated or deceptively marketed. They become victims because the TTI has manipulated decision-makers into helping them recruit their victims.

In that way, the TTI operates like a cult, and just like in a cult, when/if individuals wake up to that fact that they were part of the destruction of the psyches of young people, it can be haunting.

There are victims all around. But do you know who are not victims? The TTI facilities themselves, the private equity firms that fund them, and the educational consultants who place a child there in the first place.

Speaking of educational consultants, I met my educational consultant exactly once time before she decided my fate. And yet, she was truly the driving force behind finding the "best" option for me. I cannot prove this in my case, but I have found that many education consultants receive kickbacks from the programs they send kids to. And a lot of times, they don't even have the credentials that someone should have in this situation.

Often, the way I explain it is to ask someone, "Do you think mental health is important?"

"Of course," they say, "Absolutely."

Then I ask, "Do you think it's fair to say that mental health is health?"

Again they'll say, "Yes, absolutely, mental health is health."

So I say, "Do you think it would be weird if I had chest pain and I went to the ER, for the ER doctor to take one look at me and say: 'We have to do surgery right now'? He doesn't want to do any tests, but he wants to do surgery. Maybe I relent and say, 'Okay, we'll do the surgery. Where's the heart surgeon? I'm scared.' To which he says, 'No, no, no. I got it. I got this covered.'"

The ER doctor who thinks he is a heart surgeon is the equivalent to the role of the educational consultant. Except when people die in a hospital, things are different. There is follow-through. There are regulations and surveys. Things we don't come close to doing for mental healthcare. We are not figuring out what's at the root of the problem. Instead, we send kids away.

There always need to be diagnostic tests before you treat someone especially when the treatment itself can cause trauma.

Let's stay with the heart surgeon analogy.

If your kid has heart surgery, of course you're waiting to make sure she or he is okay. If they're not, you're going to find out they're not and be there for them.

My parents made a decision with this educational consultant and they took a leap of faith, and waited to talk to me to make sure I was okay, both at the hospital and at Chrysalis. But every chance I had to tell them I wasn't okay was monitored. There was staff on the phone. This happened to everyone there. You're not really able to say if you're okay or not because the people who are truly in charge of your well-being are listening in. If they detect any challenges brewing, these programs will hang up the phone. Then, they'll contact the parents and tell them you are lying. They'll talk about how this kind of behavior is very normal in the beginning.

At best, educational consultants and facilities directors are unqualified, at worst, they are hazardous. These people purposefully take over children's lives and often destroy them. The question is, why?

There are undoubtedly psychological issues with control and power at play. But there's also money. While young me didn't have a clue about the drivers of the TTI, there were plenty of red flags that older me recognized later.

The husband-and-wife team that ran Chrysalis at the time I was there were named Kenny and Mary. Kenny had a big boat that he'd take us out on. I can't even imagine the insurance premiums that cover having a girls' home with a boat and taking everybody water skiing or snow skiing every weekend. Then we started going on international trips. Kenny and Mary didn't pay for the trips; our parents paid extra for the trips.

Chrysalis cost about $10,000–$12,000 a month back in 2001, which roughly translates to $17,000–$20,000 in 2023. When you are almost guaranteed to be there for over a year, that is a lot of money. I've known countless survivors whose parents took out a second mortgage on their home to be able to send their kid away to a TTI facility.

Meanwhile, while I was at Chrysalis, Kenny and Mary bought a Camaro as well as a second house in Whitefish, Montana.

Then, as Chrysalis grew, they had to purchase a second house down the road to expand the amount of space to keep girls. Having more students leads to more buildings being built all over the property, which greatly enhanced its resale value. Then, Kenny got his pilot's license and his own plane—a Cessna.

Finally, after selling Chrysalis to Innerchange, I'm told this couple purchased a place in Mexico.

Meanwhile, the rest of us have had to spend the rest of our lives picking up the pieces.

Chapter Four

HERE, I DON'T FEEL LOVED

I was at Chrysalis, a "school" that was really a behavioral modification program, for my final three years of high school. At the time, it was a small, private program owned by Kenny and Mary, who doubled as our therapists. Kenny, Mary, and the girls who were in Chrysalis all lived together in a big log cabin in the middle of the woods.

We lived north of a very remote northern Montana city called Eureka, population 993, give or take. It was 14 miles to the nearest gas station, the nearest anything, with long and remote, windy and hilly roads to get you there. There was nothing you could run to, even if you wanted to run. If you went north, you would hit the Canadian border in just a couple of miles, and in town, you were monitored—everyone knew you as a "Chrysalis girl" and would report back to Kenny and Mary if you did anything out of the ordinary while in public.

I had been thrilled by the possibility of getting out of the hospital, but on the day I actually arrived at Chrysalis I remember wishing I could go back.

We could say the grass is always greener or that the hospital was the devil that I knew, but really it was about the mounting trauma. Even though lockdown was a place I couldn't hate more, that environment became one I almost trusted and looked back on fondly. My feelings of familiarity and routine lived there. Now I was being dropped off at a place where I had no idea what was going on, or why I was there, and it felt like danger all over again. When I eventually went on to college, my refrain progressed to, "I wish I were back in Chrysalis." These are the continuing fruits of unaddressed trauma.

I arrived at Chrysalis in the middle of the night. Usually, when girls arrive, they go directly to the Chrysalis house, but I was one of the few girls who ever arrived on the very first night of their yearly "service trip" in Glacier National Park. That meant I didn't arrive at any house, I arrived at a tent.

It was 1 or 2 a.m. when I got to their campsite, and everyone was asleep. It was pitch black, and someone just pointed in the dark, saying, "Your tent is over there." I literally couldn't see where they were pointing, but I walked in the general direction. I bumped into seemingly everything on my way, shuffling my feet on the ground with my arms stretched out in front to ensure I didn't trip over anything. When I finally arrived at my supposed tent, I climbed in and unrolled my sleeping bag. I had no idea who else was in there. I had no choice but to try to just go to sleep.

That trip was a microcosm of my entire stay and set the tone for the next three years.

As I mentioned, I had gained 60 pounds in the hospital. I used to be a really good athlete, but now I was in no shape to do hard, physical work for 10–12 hours a day. They called it a service trip, but what I experienced was forced, unpaid child labor.

For 70–80 hours that week, we built turnpikes over muddy sections of trails to protect horses from getting stuck. We hauled 50-pound bags of gravel, 10–20 in a row, to fill in those turnpikes. We built switchback trails straight up mountains through overgrown brush. We placed culverts in areas of the trails that needed better drainage. This is the only reason I know what a Pulaski is—an axe with a blade on one side and a pick on the other—because I had to use one for countless hours.

We did work that grown men would struggle to do, and we were expected to do it flawlessly. I don't think these are normal things for a 15-year-old to know how to do, and if you factor in that I was not getting as much food as I was used to, of course, it makes sense that I complained. But no one was allowed to complain. If you did, you would be called dramatic, a label that would stick with me for my entire time there.

At the end of the week, we had to do a 14-mile day hike right off Going-to-the-Sun Road. Seven miles in, so halfway through, we came to this big hotel where there was a switchback. As we made our way up the mountain pass, I became fucking tired. My heart was beating out of my chest. My legs felt like jelly. Halfway up this huge switchback, I felt like I had to take a break. So I did, standing there bent over, huffing and puffing with my hands on my knees.

Then, out of nowhere, a bear appeared with its cub looking extremely protective.

Everyone was shouting at me, "You need to move! Go! Go! Go!"

I cried, "I can't! I'm going to die right now, I can't breathe!"

They just kept saying, "You need to move!"

The bears were even closer now. One of the other girls, Julia, took my pack to help me. I simply couldn't handle that very heavy backpack on top of all the extra weight I was carrying at the time.

With Julia's help, I made it up the hill safely without becoming bear food.

That event became something I would never live down for my three years at Chrysalis. *Remember that time that you almost got us attacked by a black bear because you were too lazy?* It became the framework for everything that I needed to change. I needed to change how I let my insides out so that the way I felt was not always displayed on my face. I couldn't wear my heart on my sleeve any longer. If I was suffering, if I was dealing with things, I could never talk about it.

Stuck on Level One

Back then, Montana was a very popular state for TTI facilities. The endless acres of wilderness had a vacation-like feel, so TTI programs were billed as more of a retreat than anything else. But what really allowed so many institutions to flourish there was that for the longest time the regulations that governed them fell under the Department of Labor and Industry.

The Department of Labor is better suited to things like workers' comp and issuing professional licenses. I mean, they regulate weights and measures in commercial transactions; they should never have been overseeing operations and safety for youth programs in the first place.

It would take almost 20 years for residential programs in Montana to come under the supervision of the Department of Public Health and Human Services. Before that, there was no real oversight for these so-called "therapeutic programs."

Montana programs were advertised as a place where children could challenge themselves by utilizing the beautiful wilderness landscapes the state offers in order to get back to who they truly are. In reality, they were just behavior modification programs designed to break children through excessive rules, punishments, physical endurance activities, and attack therapy. (Attack therapy goes by many different names in programs, but in Chrysalis they called it "Circle"). These programs just so happened to be located in the wilderness.

The rules and level systems at Chrysalis were very confusing. To make matters worse, when I attended, there were no handouts or orientations to be able to reference while learning the ropes. You arrive and are thrown into the thick of it. Navigating the Chrysalis rules was like being handed a Rubik's Cube in the dark and told to solve it with no instructions. It was the kind of puzzle that would make escape room enthusiasts rethink their life choices.

When I first arrived at Chrysalis, I was homeschooled. I use that term very loosely, because I do not think I ever had any instructional lessons by licensed teachers during this time. It consisted of being handed lessons and a textbook, and letting the staff know when you are ready for a quiz/test. Along with every new arrival, I was placed on something called Level One, which basically means they didn't trust you at all.

Level Ones were not allowed to be without a staff member at any time. I also had to abide by all kinds of silly rules that had to be followed by everyone in order to progress to the next level and show that you were "working." We were not allowed to have milk, unless they said we were and then it was only one glass. If you drank it without permission, you would be placed on a "milk ban." If you left out an item overnight in the common areas and forgot to take it to your room, it went to "jail." It didn't matter if it was your winter jacket and it was 40 degrees outside—you didn't get that item out of jail without doing a consequence like chopping wood, in the freezing cold, without a coat.

Each level came with a specific set of privileges, and it was up to you to stay in that privilege set and not exceed it, or you were punished. With each level progression you got more privileges, which obviously enticed and incentivized you to want to progress forward. I almost saw the level system as a ladder to humanity. With every rung passed, you were treated more and more like a human and closer to getting out.

For instance, on Level One, you could only wear foundation and mascara, as far as make-up is concerned, but you couldn't wear eyeliner. No way—eyeliner and eyeshadow came with Level Two, so don't do that!

On Level One, you also couldn't talk to your parents without having a staff member on the phone. All contact with your parents was monitored; there was no way to have any kind of autonomy. Private phone conversations with your parents weren't allowed until level 3.

I remember a 30–50-minute phone call once a week where Kenny or Mary were always on the phone with me. I was never dumb enough to try to say something negative on the line, but I knew of other times when people tried to say they weren't getting enough food, or they had to work all the time, or they wanted to go home. When that happened, Kenny or Mary would end the call and get upset with the girl. Then, they would call the parents back and say, "I warned you that this kind of manipulation would happen …."

When you got to Level Two, you were potentially allowed to attend Lincoln County High School in town. That didn't happen for me until eleventh grade. For my junior and senior years, I was in a public high school setting for school hours, but I still had to abide by the Chrysalis rules while I was there, and then after school, I'd go home to Chrysalis.

Then, on Level Three, you were already going to the local high school and as an added bonus you were allowed to have a boyfriend.

Level Threes were also allowed to go home for things like Thanksgiving and finally have conversations with your parents without having staff listening in at all.

I couldn't wait to move up from Level One and enjoy a bit more freedom. In the meantime, not being allowed to have any kind of real conversations with my parents—all of the experience, really—was traumatic. I knew we had our issues, but I missed home. I missed my bed. I missed California. Most of all—at both Chrysalis and the hospital—I missed feeling loved.

I went a good four years not being around love and not feeling love from the people I loved at home.

Here is a sample journal entry from those days:

"I don't really know what to say because nothing happened today. I guess I can talk about how I'm homesick. I really miss my mom. That's really weird, though, because my mom and I aren't too close. Usually, I only miss my dad because we're close.

"My mom sent a fax with a picture of smiley faces and a baby kitty in the letter, that made me miss her. I guess I'm starting to realize that she loves me so much more than I understand. I used to think they didn't like me because they keep sending me away. It really feels good knowing people love you, but it's hard living in a house where you don't feel loved.

"Here, I don't feel loved. I don't really get hugs or anything like at home. At home, I'm told: 'I love you' before I go to school, and even though I hadn't appreciated it in the past, I'm just missing it now."

Chrysalis could not help me with these feelings. In fact, the feedback I received when they insisted on reading my journals often made me feel worse. For example, if I wrote in my journal, "I wish I could feel more love in my life," Mary would write back in red something like, "Well, I wonder how you can change to be better able to receive love." That didn't help me when I had to spend holidays away from my parents. Or my birthday came and went, and I couldn't be with my family.

During this time my father also took a new job in Chicago. So, my parents moved from my familiar home when I wasn't even there, and that was really hard. I think it would have made it easier to go through what I went through if I could have retained a connection to where I lived, to remember the place and know that I was going to go back there again sometime.

Instead, at Chrysalis, it was like I had no home. From the moment I got sent away, I lost everything. There were no friends I was able to keep in contact with. Everything I knew was gone.

So what kind of kid does that make? Someone who is hypervigilant about nothing being permanent. That is what created my anxiety. I never had anxiety as a kid. I had anxiety after this.

What's in a Name

I think I'm lucky to have gone by Mary in the hospital because it allowed me to keep that experience neatly stored away in a little box removed from myself. That was only for six months, though. My persona as "Lizzy" lasted at Chrysalis for three years. After a while, it became hard to distinguish where Meg ended and Lizzy began. Unfortunately, the changing of my name in this circumstance couldn't protect me from the hurt and eventual indoctrination I experienced.

My journey towards becoming indoctrinated seems so wild now. It took a long time for me to determine how it even happened to me.

My opinion on the process is that it all started with them labeling and categorizing who you are as being inherently bad or wrong. Then, once you feel absolutely broken, they swoop in to be the one to pick up the pieces by offering love and the tools to help you get better—the Chrysalis program. That's when they have you right where they want you, and they keep you there by having an endless number of rules to exert the utmost control and break you down.

Lizzy had problems.

Lizzy was dramatic.

Lizzy was intrusive and abrasive.

Lizzy didn't have friends.

Lizzy was this and that.

As I became increasingly brainwashed, as I became more moldable, I would start to act more in the ways they wanted me to. Any time I would start reverting back to old ways, they would compare and contrast me to my old self to make sure I didn't go back there.

In my journals, I can see Mary talking about "Old Lizzy" versus "New Lizzy." It was like she wanted me to believe Old Lizzy was dead, but new Lizzy had a chance to succeed in this world. There was also this notion that if it weren't for Chrysalis, this new Lizzy never would have occurred. I clearly remember the sense of gratitude that was instilled and expected. I went along with it because of my need to feel loved.

Ironically, I never worried I was going back to being the old Lizzy—the indoctrination had set in that far. My worries were only, *Oh god, if I make a mistake, they're going to start not liking me again.*

It always seemed to me like if Mary and Kenny could find an area where they could exert control, they would seize it. It didn't matter how small.

For example, you weren't allowed to listen to CDs when you were on Level One. And we were never allowed to listen to rap. We were told that rap represents the wrong set of ideals and morals, as it relates to "gang culture." We couldn't even listen to Christian rap. So, even if it was a white person rapping about Jesus, it didn't matter. Furthermore, they had no problem with us listening to The Grateful Dead, who were notoriously "pro-drug culture." That's how attached they were to their views on the world.

If you didn't adapt to their views, you didn't progress in the program. So you adapted.

We weren't allowed to read any romance novels.

We were not allowed to watch R-rated movies, even if you were 17 or 18 and still living there.

They even controlled the clothes we wore. Your shorts had to be below your fingertips, which is actually really hard to find. (This was before Bermuda shorts were popular; a lot of girls resorted to wearing board shorts.) You couldn't wear tank tops or anything with spaghetti straps. The clothing over your shoulder had to be at least two-and-a-half inches wide. And you could forget about anything that showed any kind of cleavage or a bathing suit that wasn't a one-piece.

Sexuality, in general, was highly controlled at Chrysalis. You were not allowed to be openly gay. However, you couldn't have heterosexual crushes either. If you talked about the opposite sex too much, they would criticize that.

One time in my journal, I wrote about a boy at school that I had a crush on. His name was Derek. (This was in my second year at Chrysalis when I had finally moved onto the coveted Level Two and I was allowed to go to high school. But I was not at Level Three and therefore not allowed to have a boyfriend yet.) In my journal I go on to describe how Derek asked for a kiss, but I said no; I even wrote him a letter to set a boundary because that's what I had been instructed to do.

Despite this, Mary scrawled in the margins: "I know you don't believe Derek is interfering with school, but he is taking up a lot of your time. Thinking about him, writing him letters, sharing letters to him with others, and so on. I appreciate that you are respecting the rules. I question if you should be innocent friends with this guy at all. He smokes weed, and that automatically makes him not approved as a friend. You need to be picking friends with clean, sober, mostly healthy lifestyles."

Ironically, Mary had no problem with a majority of the girls continually focusing on, bidding for, and fighting over Kenny's attention and love. This element of control was likely the most difficult to work through later on in life.

The amount of favoritism Kenny showed was highly traumatic, and there was a constant fight to get his attention and stay in his good graces. The way he showed this affection also had a strong influence on my future decisions and partners in life.

When Kenny was happy with you, he would come up behind you and grab the back of your neck with one hand and squeeze. Hard. Doing this would both hurt and feel good at the same time because, despite the pain it caused, you knew it meant he was happy with you. If you were lucky enough to sit next to him in the front seat of the suburban or van, he would also do this slap technique on your leg where he would squeeze that area right above your knee that is very ticklish.

When I first arrived, Kenny—who was around six foot three inches tall—also loved to wrestle the girls and have wrestling matches. Writing this out is even traumatic because it now feels so... ick ... but these were my favorite times because they allowed me an opportunity to impress Kenny with my strength.

Believe it or not, it wasn't until I had my first child and started watching her grow up that I realized how inappropriate it was that Kenny, who I was supposed to share a therapeutic relationship with, appeared to enjoy wrestling with his patients. I only woke up to this fact because I would ask myself, "Would I want my daughter or son doing this?"

Eventually, something happened, and Kenny stopped wrestling with us and then only watched us wrestle each other. I was told by another girl at the time that there was a girl who made some allegations behind the scenes, and Kenny was very upset. We were never told the allegations, but I remember Kenny telling us that he wasn't allowed to wrestle with us any more and he said it was because someone was "making up lies."

What is it about sexual repression, romantic repression, or relational repression that forms such an important part of control over a teenage girl? I think it was about influence. It appeared to me that they wanted to have 100 percent control, and that meant control over who or what was influencing you.

If a girl had feelings for someone, a boy, or another girl, she would be influenced in some way by those feelings. Chrysalis claimed that any kind of relationship—or even an attraction—would divert you from your focus, which should be on your treatment plan and getting better. In reality, I think they were more scared that an outside influence would affect their stronghold over us.

Not being able to go through the normal rites of passage created trauma. I never got to properly date a boy in high school. We were allowed to go to prom, but not with a boy. They had to okay the dress and you had to be home at a certain time. You couldn't dance with a guy, flirt with a guy, or touch a guy in any way.

Approved and Unapproved

When Mary told me that Derek, a short-lived high school crush, was "not approved," she was referring to lists that Kenny kept of the "approved" and "unapproved" people in your life. I don't know if there ever was an actual list, but the implication was that there was.

If someone at the high school had ever done anything that was against Kenny's morals, then you couldn't talk to them. If they'd ever been known to go to parties or consume alcohol or drugs, you couldn't talk to them. You had to act like they didn't exist while you were at school.

This could also apply to your own family members.

If Kenny and Mary decided that one of your family members was not a good influence on you, they would not let you write to them, and they would monitor all mail coming in to intercept anything.

This is where the parallels with being in a cult become just too obvious to ignore. It was already weird enough that they wanted to be thought of as our parents. That was the way Chrysalis was originally described to me—that there was a program where there was this mom and dad. So you don't have to worry about not going home because it's going to be just like home for us.

Kenny and Mary were the father and mother figures, and we were all "sisters." That mentality played a large role in our believing that it was okay, even normal, to sit on Kenny's lap because he was just kind of like your dad. It's not weird to wrestle a full-grown man, because he's my Chrysalis family.

Even after you have graduated from the program and receive the highly coveted Chrysalis ring they only give to graduates, you're always considered family. However, you only remain family if you continue to make good decisions after leaving Chrysalis.

I am definitely no longer an approved Chrysalis girl.

If you're in college and you're drinking—even if you're over 21—you're not allowed to visit Chrysalis. You're on the unapproved list, even though you have a Chrysalis ring.

If you have sex while you're in Chrysalis? If you run away? You're kicked out, and now you have to figure out a way to finish high school.

Kenny made a point of saying, "There are no bolts and chains on these walls. Chrysalis girls are expected to stay in their beds."

That was a big thing we always heard. If you left your bed you were threatened with things like, "You will leave Chrysalis. You will go to some other program. You will never be welcome back." That was scary in and of itself. I saw many girls be sent to other programs that were described to us as "worse."

We had these Chrysalis sisters that we were bonded to, whom we called sisters, but if they made a mistake where they were kicked out of Chrysalis, we had to excommunicate them. Kenny would flip a switch, and we were never allowed to talk positively about them anymore. I saw it happen many times, where a girl well-loved by Kenny made a mistake, and all of a sudden, she's done.

I remember one time in 2002 we took a road trip to the Grand Canyon. While driving through the Southwest we stopped at a campsite outside of Taos, New Mexico, for the night. One of the new girls who had just arrived from a wilderness program ran away in the middle of the night. No staff even noticed until morning when the girls got up and noticed she was missing.

I remember Kenny saying to the girls, "Well, I called the authorities, so there's nothing more we can do! Let's pack up and get out of here!"

I never saw that girl again, and we left her there. I feel sick remembering this because I can't imagine how her parents felt as this girl's "legal guardians" drove off, leaving her in the middle of New Mexico with no money, no ID, and no shelter in the middle of the summer heat.

We were all family until someone crossed an unforgivable line, and then we weren't family any longer.

Chapter Five

LIZZY, YOU'RE DOING IT AGAIN

After nine long months I finally got my Level Two and was able to attend Lincoln County High School in town.

When people find out I attended a public high school while at Chrysalis, they often ask me: "You were out in public, unsupervised, and you didn't try to run?!" They are asking about flight, one of the possible responses to abuse in addition to fight, freeze or fawn.

No, I never ran. It didn't even occur to me as an option to try.

First of all, you have the other Chrysalis girls at school watching your every move. If you speak to or even look at anyone else who might be able to help you, they are most likely on the unapproved list, and then you are going to be confronted and possibly lose a level.

Secondly, even though I didn't know it at the time, my autism actually made the "not running" very easy. In true autistic fashion, I stayed super morally rigid to the "Chrysalis rules." I would never have risked something if the possible result was a loss of a level, or worse, falling out of the good graces of Kenny and Mary.

I wasn't going to mess with that.

Your level was everything. In fact, you were even referred to that way. "Today, all the Level Ones are going to ...." Or, "Nope, only Level Twos can do that!" It was our social hierarchy—which meant everything to me as I felt like an outcast—and every level brought me closer to freedom. Unlike in the hospital, where you can gain and lose a level regularly, at Chrysalis, it took me those nine difficult months to get my Level Two. That is a long time commitment and a lot of pain to bargain with along the way.

Also, when people say, "Why didn't you just leave?" I think they're not quite understanding the level of conditioning I had been subject to.

By the time I reached Level Two I was completely brainwashed into thinking Chrysalis was a great program. Whether it was due to being on the spectrum or pure naiveté, I didn't have the social awareness yet to understand that what I was going through was abuse. My overall experience felt bad because I was not accepted, but it never once crossed my mind that this wasn't the way it was supposed to be.

Sometimes I look back and remember my blind trust faltering. I can be very strong-willed, so there were times where I wouldn't agree with what they were saying. I might even say, "This isn't fair." But my questions always got me accused of being manipulative. They used that word as a weapon against us and also encouraged us to use it against our peers.

You're crying because you're homesick? That's manipulative.

You're cringing in pain after an injury? Manipulation.

You wrote too many letters home or received too many letters or packages? Manipulation.

You innocently asked a staff member for something that you were completely unaware wasn't okay? "Lizzy, you're doing it again. You're doing it again! Lizzy! Lizzy! Lizzy!"

So I would think, *Fuck! Fine.*

It is a breaking of the spirit.

It's the learned helplessness again, the rat still pushing that damn button with its nose to get its electric shock because nothing matters. Hell, the electric shock was even starting to feel good.

That's really how they worked their magic on me. They stripped away who I thought I was by making me question my reality and everything I thought I believed about myself.

They had made a promise to my parents that they would "get me into shape." What my parents didn't know was that they planned on doing it through any means necessary. My parents didn't know that process involved breaking down my ideals and values to make room for the Chrysalis tools. They didn't know it involved molding me into who Chrysalis thought I should be instead.

When I was given that toolbox, I thought, *Okay. I feel so crappy right now I'm going to go ahead and use these tools because they are the only ones that I have.* Maybe the proper use of a tool would come with a little gift—a gift of something that never should have been taken away in the first place—love and acceptance.

Their brainwashing meant I ceased to see the bigger picture. My sense of the horizon began to dim. And nowhere did the brainwashing take place more than at Circle.

Thank You for Your Feedback

One of the most traumatizing experiences during Chrysalis happened during something called "Circle." Circle was Mary and Kenny's version of group therapy, although it followed none of the supportive or respectful guidelines you may be familiar with where "group" is concerned. In reality, it is just another clever name for what is known as "attack therapy," mentioned earlier. Attack therapy refers to a controversial and largely discredited psychotherapeutic approach that encourages individuals to express repressed emotions through aggressive or confrontational means, with the aim of helping people achieve emotional catharsis and insight.

Before I woke up, I had lost many memories of my time in Chrysalis, but Circles had been etched directly onto my soul. They left a deep scar that had a throughline in future relationships or friendships. For a long time the experience made it almost impossible to receive any kind of feedback from any friend or loved one without my defenses going up immediately. As soon as it is apparent in a conversation that I have done something wrong and someone is calling me out, I shut down immediately and become very defensive. It also naturally made me very hypercritical in my relationships with people.

Here's how Circle worked. Four nights a week, you had to go into the main part of the house, where the kitchen and the living room were located. Some of the girls would hurry to the couches so they wouldn't be forced to sit on the floor. Some would sit on those Crazy Creek chairs, the kind that people usually take camping because they are portable and fold up easily.

Most of the girls arrived at Circle clutching some kind of support item to help them through. Several had their hoodies up and tied to help them feel invisible, others had wrapped blankets around themselves tightly. The girls on the couch might have hold of a blanket and be anxiously wrapping their fingers around the tassels on the fringe because Circle was the time to bring up to your peers your views of how they were doing. The fringe of every blanket on that couch was knotted and worked down because of this. I know this, because the self-soothing habit I developed was trying to detangle them.

We had cats and dogs on the property, so sometimes the dogs would be in there, and you'd be petting them, or maybe the cat would be lying on you while you were thinking, *I hope I don't get confronted* ....

There were also always tissue boxes. There was one on each end table. They were set and ready for Circle because there were almost always going to be tears. Ironically, it's the one thing they always supplied for us without any guilt for using too many of them. They wanted and expected us to use many of them, especially in Circle. It was the ultimate tear producer, and in reality sadness was really the only emotion we were freely allowed to have in Circle. I think it was because it was a sign that they broke you.

There are three fates, or options, for those who are in Circle. The confronter, the confronted, and the hider. Most girls who were "working the program" came in planning to be the confronter, that is, bring up an issue with someone that hopefully Mary and Kenny would find appropriate and then confront them in front of their peers.

If you planned to be the confronter, you had a bit of a different feeling walking into Circle, though things could turn on you at any given time. If you were not the confronter, then you were walking into Circle anxiously hoping your name wouldn't get called. These were the girls who perhaps had a hard week or knew they might have complained more than usual. If the best-case scenario unfolded and your name didn't get mentioned then you had effectively shielded yourself for one night. You had hidden in plain sight.

The tension in the air at Circle was always unmistakable.

No one wanted to be there.

First, Kenny and Mary would make a few announcements, and maybe issue a few general criticisms or generalized complaints about the entire house. Then Kenny would say, "Okay, so who wants to go first?" and the feeling of anticipation would build to a fever pitch.

It felt eerily similar to what I imagine it would be like on a pirate ship, waiting your turn to walk the plank into shark-infested waters. You want to park it on that plank for as long as possible because as soon as you hear someone speak, your heart drops, and you're thinking, *Please don't be me; please don't be me; please don't be me.* Then the second you hear your name—sudden death as you plunge into the deep.

I remember Kenny and Mary encouraging all kinds of conflict to occur in Circle, and nothing was really off limits. Looking back, it seemed that Circle was one of the most powerful forms of coercion they had because it was their form of emotional warfare to make sure no one ever felt too proud, too loved, too accepted, or too emotionally stable.

Let's say you had a run-in with someone during the week, but it wasn't even something all that serious. These are the things that happen during the week that trigger you to think, *Oh! I am going to save this for Circle!* I know it seems mean and horrible, and oftentimes I felt guilty for confronting so many girls while I was there, but it was a game they played where it was an either-eat-or-be-eaten scenario.

However, even your tactics to escape the emotional warfare could backfire, and things could flip. Let's say someone named Heather goes into Circle thinking she is going to confront someone. She says something like, "Sarah, the other day you told staff you'd finished your chores, but when I went downstairs I noticed your bathroom wasn't clean. I feel like you were being sneaky and dishonest. It makes me sad that you are not working the program."

Heather thinks for a moment that she's safe, but then, seconds later, you hear one of the girls say, "Actually, Heather, I think it's more *you* that is being sneaky because last week I saw you steal granola from the cupboard without permission."

Usually if a reverse-card gets played like that, it's extremely brutal for the one it got reversed on. Next, you'll hear someone say, "Echo," meaning they wanted to say the same exact thing. Then you hear other people repeat, "Echo." "Echo." "Echo," from all around the room. So, the person who was on the offense is now on defense. Then, over the course of the next hour or so, poor Heather would likely be held accountable for pretty much everything she had done that week to annoy anyone.

In a house full of girls, those things could be endless. Sometimes criticisms were viewed as minor, like putting away towels that were still wet when you were on laundry duty. But sometimes girls, who just so happened to be on very strong mental health medications that make you tired as hell or people suffering from depression, were eviscerated for not waking up to their alarms in the morning. It was reported to me by another survivor that in one Circle, a girl who had narcolepsy was confronted for falling asleep.

There were special types of Circles too, such as an "Accountability Circle." These ones were used to force girls to reveal things about themselves that they never should have been forced to disclose in a public way in front of their peers.

Out of respect, I do not want to go into the specifics about the things I heard girls confess in Accountability Circles, but I know that many of them were forced to do so. I am not talking about having to take ownership and admit that you were the one who snuck a glass of milk without permission, which landed everyone on a milk ban (that happened, too). I'm talking about girls being forced to recount their sexual assaults or other traumatic experiences in a way that put an unnecessary and uncomfortable amount of blame on the girls. In fact, this is how I now know I was brainwashed because I remember being proud of the girls who were "owning" their roles in their sexual assaults. Accountability circles were designed in a way to highlight our own bad decisions in the past. Even if other people had played a role in negative outcomes that harmed us, they always managed to flip the narrative in a way that forced us to take all the blame and bear all the responsibility for change. It is sickening now to recall.

Soon after arriving at Chrysalis, I was forced to read my life story to everyone in Circle, and Kenny asked me to talk about how one time my Dad had gotten so angry with me that he grabbed my arm and threw me onto the bed, as a way to get me out of the way. It was in no way something I would consider abuse, and I didn't think this scenario had a significant meaning to my life, nor did I think it was something I needed to talk about. Kenny disagreed with me and thought it was relevant and that I needed to tell the story.

During the Circle where I had to tell my story, Kenny turned to me and said that because my father had done that, he would be cautious in his relationship with me because he didn't want to trigger me in any way. I think he wanted me to tell that story to have a documented excuse as to why he never liked me or got close to me in any way. He needed a reason as to why he consistently made me feel like a relationship with him was unattainable.

One of the reasons that programs like Chrysalis are able to get some traction is because they're taking the predominant emotional need of an age group—in this case, teenagers and their need to belong—and turning it against them. The need for belonging is crucial in that developmental stage, and what better way to emphasize the need for belonging than to cast someone else out? This is why TTI faculty didn't have to work too hard to encourage teenagers to gang up on each other and bully each other, whether they were girls or boys.

Even in the thick of being brainwashed, it seemed unnatural to me that part of growing up was hearing your friends say really horrible things about you. Here was this "therapeutic process" that had inherent hurt and pain intertwined into the very fabric of its existence. If that's what friendship, life, and being an adult are about, it's depressing.

Circles were incredibly rough for me. The worst feeling in the world was when I heard my name mentioned. It was a sinking feeling, where my anxiety and dread turned into a giant ball of despair stuck somewhere between my chest and my throat. It made it hard to breathe. I felt this utter hopelessness knowing it was going to be another few hours of hearing everything I was doing wrong and there was nothing I could do to stop it.

It was a very similar feeling to being on a roller coaster, strapping yourself in, and being ratcheted up that steep slope to make your first free fall. With every inch you gain going up that slope, you feel more and more of the anticipation, the anxiety, the fear, and the utter regret and desire to get off the ride; but it is too late. Your fate has been sealed.

It was later corroborated by many girls who attended Chrysalis at the same time as me that I took up a lot of Circle time. There were a lot of Circles talking about what Lizzy could change and what Lizzy needed to do better. The girls later displayed genuine compassion as to how difficult that must have been for me at the time. I just wasn't the type that could "slide under the radar."

It was difficult getting confronted by people who you know are doing better than you. That hurts more than just realizing you're not doing well. And it would always be couched in a sugar-sweet construction like, "Lizzy, I've been really frustrated. You've been really intrusive in conversations. I won't be talking to you and you'll comment and it's really starting to get on my nerves. I feel like it's inappropriate when you do that. My hope for you is that you can learn how to better understand the boundaries of conversations. My hope for myself is that I can have more patience with you as you learn these things."

Meanwhile, I had to just sit there. I couldn't say anything.

I learned that the hard way.

I couldn't come back and say, "I can understand why you're thinking that, but that's not my intention," or "I don't feel like that's the case at all. I haven't once interrupted any of your conversations this week."

If you did try to explain your actions, Kenny or Mary or another girl would say something like, "Lizzy, I feel like you're being defensive. I feel like you should just take the feedback in." So basically, you just had to sit there.

Then, despite the prominent tissue boxes, your crying was seen as anything but sadness in others' eyes. They might say, "You're being really dramatic right now," or "You're playing the victim." So then you had to try to repress your emotions unless that emotion was the sadness of pure defeat. Beyond crying, you had to make sure your face was void of any other movements to suggest you were frustrated. No furrowed brows, passive-aggressive smiles or looks, eyerolls, or deep breaths. It was just tears or nothing at all in Circle. And at the end, all you could say was something like, "Thank you for your feedback."

Fuck Around and Find Out

Daisy was an incredibly bright young woman who was about to graduate from Chrysalis. She had a full-ride scholarship to a Christian college and was two semesters away from graduating Lincoln County High School at the top of her class. She was on Level Three, which meant she was allowed to have a boyfriend.

One day Daisy and her boyfriend (who was on Mary and Kenny's approved list) had sex and, while they didn't get caught in the act, Daisy became pregnant.

Daisy found out she was pregnant when she suffered a medical emergency while flying back from a home visit and made the hard decision that she wanted an abortion. She tried to do the right thing by telling Kenny and Mary.

This is where things turned catastrophically for Daisy.

In true Chrysalis fashion, immediately after learning that Daisy had not only had sex but intended to have an abortion, Kenny and Mary forced Daisy to come clean of her "indiscretions" to every one of her peers in an "Accountability Circle." During this Circle, her peers called her disgusting, a liar, untrustworthy, a whore, a slut, and told her that she let everyone down. These were the same people she had come to view as family and, ironically, people who were doing many of the same things she had been doing—they just hadn't been caught.

Kenny and Mary then met with Daisy and her mom, trying to convince her mom to send Daisy to a wilderness program called Second Nature—a program I now believe had a financially lucrative referral relationship with Chrysalis. When Daisy's Mom (who is disabled) refused, Kenny called her a "retard." He then assured Daisy she would end up a high school dropout and become a prostitute. He finished off by calling her a snarky little shit and told her to wipe the grin she had off her face—that he ought to slap it off of her.

Daisy's mother, in an act of protection, said, "It seems like you're trying to say there is something wrong with my daughter. Well, you had four years to fix her, and you didn't. So it seems like the problem is your program." Then she pulled Daisy from Chrysalis.

Given Daisy's success at the local high school, she moved into an apartment in Eureka to complete the school year. But soon after Daisy left Chrysalis, the university where she had been accepted revoked both her scholarship and her acceptance to the program. Daisy was told that someone had made an anonymous report of her abortion to the school and they feared she would be a "corruptive influence." Although the source of the report remains uncertain, Kenny, who was one of her references for the program, remains a likely suspect, given his knowledge of her medical history.

Despite these setbacks, Daisy tried to finish high school in town but faced isolation as her friends feared losing their "approved status" at Chrysalis if they interacted with her. Kenny had essentially put Daisy on a blacklist. Chrysalis girls were forbidden to associate with her, leaving her socially ostracized. Struggling to make ends meet with a $7.00 per hour job, she eventually moved back home to California to graduate.

While this story is specific to one person, this type of experience is representative of what I observed many Chrysalis girls go through. If girls—who seemed to have their heads on straight and had bright futures ahead—tried to challenge Kenny's authority in a way that made him or Chrysalis look bad, they potentially faced Kenny standing in between them and that future. It was a very known and understood concept that no Chrysalis girls talked about then but do now—if you fuck around with Kenny, he's going to "get even" and you're going to end up feeling his wrath in one way or another.

Fortunately for Daisy, despite what we can only assume were Kenny's best efforts to sabotage her, she went on to get a degree from a top UC school and is now a doctoral candidate at another top-ranking university.

Confronting Kenny in Circle

I certainly went toe-to-toe with Kenny, but it was much earlier in my Chrysalis career and thus didn't affect my plans for college.

Right off the bat, I felt like Kenny didn't like me. If Kenny didn't like you, he made it known.

He wouldn't look at you the same as the other girls.

He wouldn't give you compliments.

He wouldn't give you special chores to do.

He wouldn't give you special attention by tickling you or hugging you.

So, what did I do in the first Circle I participated in? I confronted Kenny.

I had only seen one Circle by that point, but I saw how people held each other accountable and thought that was what I was supposed to do. He would do the same thing to other girls. He would say what was on his mind—even if it was insulting, it didn't matter. I legitimately thought that in doing this I was doing what I was supposed to.

I was so wrong.

I said, "I don't like the way that you treat me, and I feel like you don't like me, and it makes me sad."

I really struggled with being able to name my emotions at that time. As I can read in my journal, I was either sad or I was pissed—very simple emotions. It shows how young I was. It also highlights another red flag for autism that they missed, alexithymia, or difficulty in recognizing and describing one's own emotions, which often occurs in neurodivergent individuals.

Looking straight at Kenny, I concluded with something like, "It seems like you're always mad at me."

The faces of the other girls in the circle were like, *Oh shit. I can't believe she just did that.* No one confronted Kenny. Not even Mary. If he said something, he's right. There was no other opinion.

Kenny just sat there, looking at me blankly. As I already mentioned, Kenny was a big, tall guy. He had a strong presence in the room. When he was upset, he had a very stoic look where he'd get really quiet.

While I was speaking his eyes were glassy but not so much that it looked like he was crying. They looked almost empty. You could tell from those eyes how he felt even if the words didn't match. He might be saying, "You're not making the best decisions, Lizzy." But my interpretation of his true meaning was, "You're a fucking idiot and I hate being around you." He was not able to hide his real feelings and beliefs about you and his disappointments with you.

Kenny remained very calm and let me finish, then took a deep breath, and let me have it. He told me everything I'd done wrong that week and how he didn't care what I thought because I'm the one who's got the problem and the issues lie within me, not him. He reminded me that my parent think I should be here because of this. He basically just put me in my place and made me feel like none of my feelings were valid.

But he didn't stop there. Instead, he went on the attack:

"You come off to others in a much different way than you think. You step on people's boundaries all day and are socially unaware. You're pushy, intrusive, and abrasive. You're not a good friend, and it makes people not want to be around you. If you don't change who you are and your personality, I worry you're never going to be loved or accepted in society.

"You have a chance right now to make yourself more lovable and acceptable to society, because you're only 16 and your brain isn't fully developed until you're 25. So if you work really hard, you can change who you are and your personality. Because the way you are right now is not okay."

He concluded with, "And I know you can do it. You can change who you are."

So there we had it. In that moment it was clear why I was at Chrysalis in his eyes—to learn to act differently than I was.

The Birth of the People-Pleaser

I remember feeling this immense depression after that Circle. This overwhelming feeling of not being good enough. Why was I even here on earth? Why would God make me so incapable and so unlovable—even my own birth mom didn't want me and gave me up. It must be true because Kenny said everyone around me was saying the same thing.

In a later Circle he told me, "There's a saying, if one person tells you that you have a tail you can say, 'I don't believe you' and keep on walking. But if ten people tell you that you have a tail, you might want to turn around and check."

Did I have a tail?

Would I be in this place if I didn't?

Maybe everyone was right, and I needed to change.

He made it seem like my parents were among those people who thought I had a tail. They wouldn't have sent me here if it weren't for the fact that I needed to change.

In many ways, that was a major turning point where it was ingrained in me that I would never be accepted until I was no longer me.

My parents were, and still are, the most important people in the world to me, and I have the utmost respect for them. I harbor no ill will toward them because they had no idea that my best interests weren't being supported at Chrysalis.

In Chrysalis, it never seemed like the motive was about making sure I discovered who I was and found my purpose; it felt like it was about making sure that I was "fitting into the crowd" by ensuring no one saw how weird I actually was. In Chrysalis, and most programs like it, the more you blend in the better, regardless of your individual needs. Mary and Kenny never asked, "How do you feel like you need to be supported? What can we do better?" Instead, it was constantly about, "What do you think you need to change to make others around you happier?"

And that was the birth of the people-pleaser.

You can see it in my journals, which were written in the way they wanted me to write them with the narrative I was supposed to have. At one point they shift from, "Why the fuck am I here?!" to "I'm the problem. I got upset, which means I did something wrong, and I need to change something about myself."

It was a slow shift to putting all the blame on myself. This was definitely a throughline throughout my time at Chrysalis. There was this tight rope you walk every day where you had to confront those around you to move forward, but you didn't dare do that without also taking personal accountability for all your issues or all the bad things that happened to you.

I remember feeling like the self-degradation masquerading as accountability was expected. I wrote things like, "I'm sure over the last years that my family has been very frustrated with me" and "I wish that my family never had to go through me being away from home. I wish my family never had to go through not having me." There was nothing about, *I wish I didn't have to go through this.*

At that age, when something bad happens, how do you make it better? You just apologize, right? And then it goes away. I tried to apologize for everything, including myself, because I wanted my situation to change. I thought maybe if I dug deep enough Kenny and Mary would think, "Ah! She's ready." But it never really happened. I was conditioned to empathize with everyone else and put my own needs aside; to focus on other people as though my feelings didn't matter. That conditioning literally carried over into the rest of my life as an overachiever trying to prove to the world that I was successful, that I wasn't a failure.

When my son, Jackson, was a toddler I remember he was very attached to me. His biological dad and I were divorced when Jack was only a few months old. I was both Spencer's and Jack's only parental figure for a long time, so little Jackson's need for me made sense; from his earliest memory I was his main and only caretaker.

What if I had treated Jackson's need for love and attention the way Kenny and Mary treated mine? I had that same need, seeing as I felt abandoned as well. What if I sat him down and told him he was being "needy and dramatic," then had all his grandparents and everyone who loves him tell him in a circle that they are upset with him, too, and that if he wants to continue to have our love and acceptance, he'll need to chill a little bit.

I would never treat any of my kids like that, of course. But if we aren't careful as parents, the message can still get through that they need to figure out how to adapt without love, that they need to put others first, always, and never get their own needs met. That is absolutely no environment for any child, or any human being for that matter.

Chapter Six

THINGS THAT ARE
WEIRD ABOUT ME

At that point in time, it seemed that Kenny was the only person I could trust. I thought, *He's taking care of me.*

So I made a decision.

I said to myself, "I'm going to try to do this. I'm going to try to change who I am."

Unfortunately, I wasn't changing who I was. I was actually just learning how to mask who I was. I thought I was utilizing the tools for self-help. I thought I was bettering myself, but really I was slowly starting on a path that would bring me to my knees when I entered my thirties. I started a systematic destruction of my ability to cope when I thought I was helping myself.

Looking back, it makes sense that there were a lot of Lizzy-focused Circles. To be honest, I was an easy target. I was very impressionable. And I was different, which is not something Chrysalis—or any kind of organization that flourishes under groupthink—can easily tolerate. They wanted all the girls to fit into a box and behave. But I have always told the truth. That's one of the perks of how I experience autism.

My parents always told me that I seemed unaware of the way my interactions affected others. I never understood why every time I spoke people got upset. I would come out of an exchange with someone and wonder, *Why are they upset with me? It doesn't make sense.*

There was a time I remember arguing with my father, going back and forth with him. He turned to me and said, "I wish I had a tape recorder to record the way that you talk because you have no idea how you're coming off to others."

I certainly wasn't going to develop that understanding further at Chrysalis. There, if you did something wrong, they communicated with you by giving you an extra two hours of gardening or filling wheelbarrows with rocks. They made you so scared to make a mistake that you became a perfectionist. Because of the ways I was punished back then, I became a prisoner; the mask they wanted me to wear became fully fixed to my face.

I think a lot of people in the autistic community are treated in a similar way. Our non-neurotypical behaviors may be some of the major reasons we are sent away. It's heartbreaking, actually, to look back and realize the reason that I was subjected to so much abuse was because, in effect, I wasn't "normal."

Should Chrysalis have Known Better?

Chrysalis and other TTIs claim to treat or help a myriad of disorders. The problem, of course, is that things like self-harm and suicidal ideation should not be treated in the same way as depression, or PTSD, or autism. It is absurd to claim that one setting or treatment methodology is going to be a catch-all cure. Chrysalis told me I was intrusive. They told me that I was socially off, that sometimes I was not a good friend. But they never told me why. I'm sure they didn't know I was on the spectrum. However, even if they had suspected it, or known for certain, I am not sure it would've mattered. My path would have likely been the same.

You know what's interesting? Well before I was diagnosed with autism, I taped a poem in my journal by an unknown author. It is called, "Please Hear What I'm Not Saying."[1] It starts:

Don't be fooled by me.
Don't be fooled by the face I wear
for I wear a mask; I wear a thousand masks,
masks that I'm afraid to take off,
and none of them is me.
Pretending is an art that's second nature with me,
but don't be fooled,
for God's sake don't be fooled.
I give you the impression that I'm secure,
that all is sunny and unruffled with me, within as well as without,
that confidence is my name and coolness my game
that the water's calm and I'm in command
and that I need no one,
but don't believe me.
My surface may be smooth, but my surface is my mask ....

I don't remember putting that in there, but I know they read my journals religiously. Were there really not enough clues to put together what was really going on with me?

While at Chrysalis, a new girl named Cara arrived. She never ran; she always galloped like a horse. While I will never know for certain, I look back and feel that Cara was autistic. Even if I didn't know the terminology of the spectrum yet, I knew she was different. I knew she processed information differently. I knew the way

---

1 This poem, which circulated for decades with an "author unknown" credit, was later claimed by the poet Charles C. F nn: https://poetrybycharlescfinn.com/pages/please-hear-what-im-not-saying

she interacted socially was different, and she struggled greatly there because she was expected to be like everyone else. She was socially ostracized and bullied for many things. From what I saw, she never seemed to receive any kind of accommodations and was held to the exact same standards as everyone else.

In these programs in the TTI, if something is wrong with you and they are not equipped to treat or help that condition, it means you will need special care. However, that costs money for more staff, either in-house or to transport you for outpatient services. That, in addition to the homogenization that all cult-like environments require, is why they needed everyone to require the exact same level of care, consistently.

The same concept applied to medical care. If a staff member left the property to take someone to the hospital, the ratio changed. Then they needed to pay an additional person to stay compliant with state regulations. This is on top of the fact that when you have 30 teenage girls on the property, they're going to need normal checkups, vaccinations and dentist visits. On top of that, a lot of them are on medication so you will also have visits to psychiatrists.

Put all this together, and you can see how it would be preferable to hold on to the illusion that—no matter what our needs—we were all faking it. That was why Kenny's first response to every illness or injury, no matter how dire, was, "Nothing's wrong with you, you're fine."

Finding Out I was Autistic ... from TikTok

This is going to seem pretty crazy but hang with me. Before I went for an extensive battery of tests, I initially found I was autistic by watching TikTok videos.

I love TikTok, and during the pandemic, I watched a ton of it. For those who aren't familiar with this addictive app, the way TikTok's algorithm works is by aggregating data about you including what sorts of things you type into the search bar, what kinds of things you watch, and for how long. Then, they will curate TikTok's content for you.

You might see a video that says, "Chances are, if you're watching this, you believe in critical race theory and teaching your kids the right things to say. You also try your hardest to not be racist ...." The theory is if you end up on a certain side of TikTok, chances are you're there because you've been seeking that kind of content, even if subconsciously.

When I first joined TikTok, I mostly sought entertainment and learned how to do crazy dances. Then slowly, my feed became less about entertainment and more educational. One time it showed me a video about autism, and I thought, *Oh, that's interesting*. Then I fell down a rabbit hole where I learned about the comorbidities between autism, ADHD, and trauma-related disorders, which I found really interesting.

Then the truth bombs started being dropped.

There would be videos saying things like, "To the kids who hated feeling the seam of your socks against your toes ...." Then they'd start dancing, the beat to the music would drop, and a title would come on the screen: "How's the autism treating you?"

Those kinds of videos would come up, and even though they were portrayed in a lighthearted way, to every one of them, I responded, "Oh my god, that's me!" or "That happened to me!"

But then I asked myself, "Can I really be autistic though?" I've worked with autistic people. When I was a nanny, two of the five kids I cared for had autism; at the time, I associated their higher support needs with autism and assumed this was the only way autism presented. Now my stereotypes were being called into question, but the evidence was piling up as I got answers to my questions for the first time.

I knew I had really sensitive skin and that I didn't like tags on my clothes. I can't wear anything unless it is really soft or it will really bother me. If I get my hair cut, I know I'm going to be out of sorts for the rest of the day because there is bound to be one hair still on my clothes, and I will feel it.

I'm hypersensitive—my hearing, sense of smell, touch, and taste are all acute. My physical senses bring in so much information it is almost unbearable. For the first six months of my life, I cried every time I was held. My mother had to literally wear me to get me used to physical touch.

I was scared of the dark for far longer than average (okay, I actually still am). I had issues with bedwetting until I was older. I had, and still have, a tendency that makes me mimic people's accents and facial expressions. I always interrupted people and probably came across as having minimal social awareness.

Surprisingly, most of these weren't symptoms that were necessarily connected to having ADHD (which I have always known I have). I credit TikTok for helping me put these initial pieces together.

I started putting together a page of notes on my phone, named, "Things That Are Weird About Me." I took some online quizzes and scored off the charts for high-masking autism. Yet I still wasn't ready to say, "I'm autistic." I was just trying on that hat and asking, *Does this fit? Can I think of myself in this way?* It hadn't yet become part of my identity. Because in order to do that, I'd have to transcend the stigma still attached to Autism Spectrum Disorder.

You're Fine the Way You Are

The paradox is that because of the abusive environment in both the hospital and at Chrysalis (where my autistic tendencies were harshly punished), it was that much harder to get diagnosed. The more explicitly you are taught to conform, the more neurotypical you are required to act, the tighter the mask you wear, and the more you confuse that mask with your own original face.

I don't think everyone needs to spend thousands of dollars to be assessed by a psychologist or psychiatrist to figure out if they're autistic. I think most people correctly self-diagnose whether they are on the spectrum. Ironically, it was my autism itself that caused me to need a formal diagnosis, because otherwise (according to my rigid thinking) it wasn't not true. The world of in-betweens is not my kind of world. I like definitive answers. Concrete data.

So, I made an appointment with Dr. Mark Stern, a neuropsychologist who is my therapist to this day. The assessment was spread over 20 hours of testing and took about eight weeks to reach completion. I brought him my list of *weird things about me*. He reviewed all of my symptoms, including others we discovered together.

One thing that emerged is that I watch TV and movies because they teach me about body language, the scripts of normal conversation and small talk, and how your face is supposed to look. What do you say in certain situations? I didn't know unless I could see it demonstrated for me. I always thought it was weird that watching movies was like a filing cabinet for me of how to respond with certain phrases. Especially idioms or common sayings; I didn't always understand when to use them and took them too literally. It all started to make sense.

I also learned that when you're doing an assessment, the most important thing is not so much the symptoms you have now but when did those symptoms start? If they had started when I was 15 that would most likely be due to trauma rather than autism.

My situation is complex because I am dealing with trauma as well as ADHD and Autism. I also have physical health conditions that further complicate things, such as Ehlers-Danlos Syndrome (EDS) and Mast Cell Activation Syndrome (MCAS).

It was quite a process to unravel the history of my unique set of challenges. Did I cry frequently as a baby (as my mother told me) because I was autistic and didn't want that overstimulation, or was being held irritating my skin because of Mast Cell? Or maybe my joints were hurting because of EDS? Did I not want to be held because I was just left alone for 10 days in the hospital before I was adopted? Was I suffering from residual trauma due to that abandonment?

I knew Dr. Stern was one of the best therapists I had been to after the first hour of the assessment. He is a straight shooter who seemed to get me, if that makes sense. In the first hour, he was able to tell me, even without my knowledge of it, why every other therapist I had ever had didn't work out.

"You must have a hard time finding a therapist you like, and that works, huh?" he asked as I stared back from the couch across the room.

I laughed. "I mean, I guess you could say that. What brought you to that conclusion?" I asked.

"Well, you're extremely logical, and I could see that as being something used to run logical circles around a therapist until they get confused and give up. My guess is that many therapists get stuck in a 'logic trap' with you which is a way for you to escape addressing the feelings attached to your words."

Boom! Another truth bomb. Suddenly, every relationship I had ever had with a therapist made sense.

"Wow. Yeah, that's fair. I can see that," I mustered out as I laughed hysterically.

That's when I knew that after the assessment, I was going to see if I could have him as a therapist, since he wouldn't fall for said logic trap.

While I was waiting for the results of the testing, I said to my husband, Ben, "What happens if I come back as autistic?"

He said, "Well, it would answer a lot of questions."

I also talked to my Mom and asked her, "What do you feel about the whole autism thing?"

She said, "I've been thinking about this potential diagnosis and remembering back to your childhood, and a lot of it makes so much sense. There were a lot of unanswered things, and this concretely fills in those gaps."

At the end of the day, there was an empowerment to receiving my diagnosis, though not at first. At first, I felt really, really sad. I was really sad for that 15-year-old Meg that was abused because she was different.

It's like those thought experiments you see on social media: *What advice would you give your younger self if you could?* If I could tell the 15-year-old me anything, I would say, "You're fine the way that you are."

After the initial flood of emotions, after the relief and the sadness, and the aha moments, came the next phase where I literally relived my entire life. I would imagine this is true with any diagnosis of this nature. Any experience or conversation I'd ever had that had gone really wrong, any weird things that seemingly popped up out of nowhere, it all replayed in my mind like a movie. I tried to determine: Did autism play any part in that? I had to review my history with this new lens of understanding to be able to see how I ended up where I did.

Finally, there came the work of establishing a new identity. When you get diagnosed with something like autism, it is 100 percent a new identity. I had been wearing this mask my entire life, and now I had to start understanding who was under this mask. Therapy becomes about trying to pull off that mask, as well as advocating for myself and accepting myself as who I am.

Acceptance and commitment therapy (ACT) is often a helpful type of psychotherapy for people on the spectrum, as opposed to something like cognitive behavioral therapy (CBT), which is focused on rephrasing negative thoughts that intrude. ACT is more about acceptance of the way things are rather than trying to think about things in a different way, which can be difficult owing to the rigid structures of autism. You stay focused on the present moment and accept thoughts and feelings without judgment. I started accepting anything that was making it difficult for me to survive in my own life. Accept it and move on.

That's treatment in a nutshell.

How can I understand things in a different way?

What can I add to my environment to better help me cope?

How can I better advocate for myself and my needs that I have been ignoring throughout life?

I have learned there isn't anything essentially wrong with being autistic, and believe me, that is hard to accept when years of abuse happened because of it. That is a tough concept to acknowledge and accept.

I am a TTI survivor, which means my first instinct will always be to blame myself. I was brainwashed to think that my faulty decisions alone were what would determine my destiny.

Gone are my days of being a people-pleaser who thought everything that happened to me was my own fault. I now have a much wider view of the dominoes that had to fall for my life to play out the way it did. Sometimes, others are to blame, and in my case, I had to become comfortable with placing blame where blame was due and acknowledging I deserved so much better.

Every girl at Chrysalis, regardless of their specific set of challenges, deserved so much better.

Chapter Seven

M&M'S AND A ROOT BEER FOR YOUR SILENCE

I'm going to start this chapter with a story. It's not about me, it's about another girl, one of my Chrysalis sisters, Ariel.

Ariel was fourteen years old, petite, and very fast. She ran track and field in high school and was really good. Kenny was proud of her, and from my point of view, she seemed to be one of his "favorites." That would have been typical—if you produce in his world, he is close to you, and he respects you.

One day, Ariel started noticing that her hip and leg were hurting very badly. Kenny refused to take her to an orthopedic doctor at the time, so she did what any good Chrysalis girl did—she stopped complaining. She kept running every day, until one morning she woke up and the pain was so bad, that she looked in the mirror. She noticed that, because of favoring her other leg, her injured leg was now half the diameter of her other one due to a loss of muscle mass.

She was finally allowed to go to the orthopedic doctor where X-rays revealed that she had broken her femur at the top of her hip. The doctor further explained that if the bone had been left untreated, it could have severed the artery going to her heart and killed her. She was rushed into emergency surgery without any apology from Kenny.

After a long recovery on crutches, she was finally cleared for general activity by her surgeon. This happened the same week that Kenny announced, "We're going skiing."

Ariel says, "Kenny, I just got off crutches. I don't feel comfortable going skiing."

He says, "Too bad!"

Kenny forced her onto the ski trip and told her she would be skiing black diamonds with the rest of them, since she normally was a good skier.

When Ariel was going cautiously down the mountain on her skis, fearing another injury, Kenny came up beside her and hissed, "If you don't go straight down this mountain right now, you're in big trouble."

She was so scared, but she listened to him. She skied as fast as she could down the mountain. But her muscles had atrophied after a relatively long period of inactivity, and mid-descent she heard a crack and her leg flipped out from underneath her.

Luckily someone found her, because Kenny didn't even notice. Yet despite feeling horrific pain, her first response was to tell the person she didn't need help because she didn't want to get in trouble for falling. She had to be tobogganed down the mountain and her leg was ruined, again.

Now, Kenny had to be very careful because he had made her do this. So he arranged for Ariel to return home in the Suburban with him alone. If you ever went home in the Suburban with Kenny, that was seen as a special gift. On the way home with Ariel, Kenny stopped at a gas station and bought her M&M's and a root beer, which she viewed as payment for her silence.

Upon arrival back home, he made a big show of being on Ariel's side of things and announced to the rest of the girls, "If anyone so much as touches Ariel's leg, I'm going to kick your ass."

He switched from being the cause of her downfall to being her protector in order to keep her quiet. Because she had been mind-controlled, so long as she was back in his good graces, she wasn't going to speak up.

That explained Kenny in a nutshell.

Ariel became permanently disabled from that day and has had countless surgeries on her leg; she will continue to need them yearly for the rest of her life. No surgery will ever be able to fix the damage, however, and she will never be able to walk normally again.

Physical and Emotional Wounds

The skiing accident was not an isolated incident at Chrysalis. When I tried out for the basketball team in high school, I did a layup and came down on my ankle. I heard a loud crack and crunch. I continued the two-hour tryouts even though I could barely walk.

That's what Chrysalis does to you. It pushes you to the point where you literally don't say when you're hurt because that makes you tough, and Kenny and Mary see you in a more positive light. That makes you a Chrysalis girl.

My ankle hurt for a week and then two. My foot was swelling out of my shoe. It was black and blue and swollen.

About a month later, I went to Kenny and said, "It's not a big deal ... but I still can't walk on my ankle. I'm a little scared because I did hear a pop back when I injured it, and the fact it's not better yet is kind of worrying me that something may be wrong. Do you think someone could take me to the urgent care so that we can have it checked out?"

He said, "No, absolutely not. We don't go to the doctor unless it's for a broken bone, and you can't break your ankle."

I walked away thinking to myself, *Yeah, you can. You can definitely break an ankle.* But you don't correct the man.

I completely regretted my decision to ask for help because Kenny likely now viewed me as a complainer. I remember hoping we didn't have to hear in Circle about "Lizzy being dramatic again."

So I wasn't allowed to go to the doctor for that injury, and every time we hiked, my ankle would roll. If I played soccer, it would roll. Eventually it stopped hurting, but it always remained unstable.

Many, many years later, during a massage, the massage therapist looked at how my ankle was lying on the table and asked, "Did you ever tear a tendon in your ankle?" Two weeks and an MRI later, I found out I had a four-inch tear in the peroneus brevis tendon of my ankle. I had to get it surgically repaired with a graft because of that injury that was never addressed.

In my adulthood, I have had to fix all kinds of wounds, not only emotional but also physical, from what I went through at Chrysalis.

The irony of the Chrysalis experience is that it was hyped up to be this amazing wilderness setting complete with ski trips and camping trips, as well as a ranch complete with horses that we could ride. This is one of the ways they justified the high fees that they charged to the parents. But despite these seemingly positive features, I feel like the controlling culture put the girls at continual risk of injury and subsequent medical neglect.

At one point early in my stay at Chrysalis, I was kicked straight in my lower back by one of the horses we had, named Sienna. I fell straight forward onto my face. I was shocked at first, but then the pain came, and I started screaming at the top of my lungs.

Thankfully, a staff member who really cared about us was nearby and took it seriously. She drove me an hour-and-a-half to the nearest hospital in Kalispell. The problem came when the ER doctor came up to that staff member and me after the X-ray and said, "There's nothing wrong with her, she's fine." The doctor gave me this side eye glace that indicated I was wasting the ER's time and money.

That one doctor's evaluation and subsequent determination that I was "fine" earned me the unrelenting reputation at Chrysalis for being the most dramatic Chrysalis girl. At Chrysalis, when that kind of label or stigma was placed on you; there was no point in fighting it. You own it. Therefore, I had to shut up for the next three years about my constant subsequent back pain and the shooting pains down my legs.

They even laughed about it at my Chrysalis graduation ceremony from. "Remember when Sienna kicked you in the back and you were so dramatic and pretended to be hurt?"

The problem was, I wasn't being dramatic and had actual pain and it progressively got worse through my college years, up until I was 24, when I was diagnosed with Spondylolisthesis and Spondylosis with a Pars defect. This diagnosis led to needing a double spinal fusion because my L5 (lumbosacral joint) was floating around, completely unattached.

The neurosurgeon told me, "If you had fallen over the wrong way any time in the past eight years and just bumped your rear end the wrong way (like from snowboarding which we were forced to do every weekend in winter), you could have severed your spinal cord."

Now, it doesn't necessarily take big fancy diagnostic equipment to diagnose this, but it does take the careful eye of a doctor to be able to spot it. The kicker (no pun intended) for me was that this is something that ended up being diagnosed at an urgent care through a simple X-ray. But, because the doctor at Kalispell Hospital didn't catch it, I was labeled dramatic.

The Bystander Effect

These stories are just the tip of the iceberg. With all these cases of medical neglect, you might be wondering, what about the others who worked there? Even if Kenny and Mary believed that neither illness nor injury should be treated by medicine—that ill-health was a by-product of the mind and therefore best treated in the mind by adjusting our beliefs somehow—didn't staff members have a duty to help the kids?

I recently spoke with a former staff member from Chrysalis who was there when I was there. They said they knew that we were being mistreated. They put their job on the line many times to drive us to the doctor when specifically told not to; they would often advocate for our medical needs to Kenny and Mary.

I think some staff members truly believed that because they were getting orders or directions from people who had advanced degrees or who seemed to know more about mental health than they did, it must have been an okay way to treat youth. They saw people come by and check out the program and assume that if that is being done, then the way things are must be safe otherwise they'd be shut down.

It's a version of the bystander effect, only within the context of a program. The bystander effect, also called bystander apathy, is a well-known theory that individuals are less likely to offer help to a victim when in the presence of other people.

The famous example that prompted this phenomenon was when a woman named Kitty Genovese was murdered outside her New York City apartment complex in 1964. Two weeks after the murder, the New York Times wrote an article saying that there were 38 witnesses in that apartment complex that either heard her screams or saw what was happening, but because they felt it was likely that most everyone else saw or heard it too, they didn't call the police. Everyone assumed that everyone else was taking action, so no action was taken.

While this article in the New York Times has since been labeled as having inaccuracies, because some actually did try to call the police, I do think it highlights an important piece of social psychology that is at play in this industry. The bystander effect can also apply in the macro perspective as well when looking at the government's responses to allegations of abuse in the TTI.

In 2008, the U.S. Government Accountability Office (GAO) published a report that identified thousands of abuse allegations, some of which resulted in death, at residential programs across the country. Despite the horrendous findings from this report—which recommended actions needed to protect the youth in residential programs—it took over 10 years for legislation to successfully pass any laws at the state level anywhere to help protect youth.

Returning to the Chrysalis staff, let's say that someone did realize something is off. They might even have labeled it abuse in their own minds. I know that many Chrysalis staff legitimately cared about the girls, so what do they do if they see something that they'd consider abuse? At that point, they can either report the abuse and hope for change or they could leave.

It's a Catch-22. If a staff member reports abuse, it could open up that person to potential retaliation. However, if the staff member just leaves, they're leaving the kids in an abusive situation. That thought makes it so much harder to leave, so they stay.

If you are one of the staff—you think staying with the kids is keeping them safe. Unfortunately, though, staying with them is actually keeping that job filled; whereas if all the people in the country who noticed systematic abuse quit, these facilities would be out of business. Staff staying on is inadvertently what keeps these TTI programs in business.

Everyone, at some point in time and in some capacity, has to participate in the rituals of silence for these kinds of toxic environments to exist. I myself participated in the rituals. As a result of being brainwashed, I never reported abuse either. I learned that

I would make it through Chrysalis so much faster if I just sat in the pain. It felt almost powerful to have pain and not show it. They taught me to equate the endurance of pain to being strong.

But pain should be listened to. You need to follow that pain, and let people be their own advocates, so they can communicate that pain and get help for it. Otherwise, all of those injuries will compound and become chronic illnesses.

I was fit and active as a kid. I was a flexible gymnast and soccer player, a natural-born athlete. In the years since leaving Chrysalis, I have lost a spleen, an appendix, and my tonsils. The toxic stress and abuse contributed to auto-immune disorders in my body, such as the Mast Cell Activation Syndrome (MCAS); thyroid disorders, such as Hashimoto's Disease; and cardiac disorders, such as Postural Orthostatic Tachycardia Syndrome (POTS). More recently, stomach pain led to gallbladder removal due to gallstones.

After many years of participating in the rituals of silence and accepting the narrative spun by my abusers, I finally woke up and became a member of the survivor community. It's then that I saw the patterns emerging from fellow survivors. So many of us went through years of incarceration, intimidation, belittling, and brainwashing. And another pattern that emerged from survivors in the community, is that many of us have similar diagnoses.

For context, a "rare disorder," according to the organization Rare Diseases International, is considered to be one that affects less than one in 2,000 of the population. EDS, POTS, and MCAD are all considered rare. Imagine my surprise when I became aware of the fact that those three disorders seem to occur in the survivor population at an alarming rate. In fact, I can't tell you how many survivors I have met that have all three of those disorders; it is astonishing and horrifying.

I was steeped for so long in the conditioning that "I am not good enough" and that my pain couldn't possibly be real that I thought I didn't matter enough to be helped. My self-esteem had been lowered by the abuse and culture of self-degradation in the programs. Because of that environment it's doubly difficult for survivors to stand up for ourselves and say, "That's not good enough," or even ask for help for our chronic and sometimes debilitating health issues.

Oh My God, I Killed My Dad

This pattern of denying my own pain signals came to a head on Thanksgiving day, 2002. At Chrysalis you weren't allowed to go home for Thanksgiving unless you were a Level Three, so my whole family was supposed to come up for a visit. But my brother was stuck in Boston with his job, so my mother ended up going to Boston to spend Thanksgiving with him, and my father came to spend Thanksgiving with me.

This was the year Chrysalis had expanded its bed count. With everyone's family coming in, the property was too small to host everyone, and we had to have Thanksgiving dinner somewhere else. It was going to be held at the Baptist Church in Eureka; my father and I were coming from Kalispell, which is about an hour and 15 minutes away.

The route from Kalispell to Eureka is basically a long stretch of highway with woods on both sides. The speed limit in Montana was 75 MPH in those days. I did not yet have my driver's license, only a learner's permit. That meant I could only drive with another licensed driver in the car, in this case, my Dad, and I was getting some practice in his rental, a Pontiac Montana minivan.

There were tons of deer and elk known to roam those highways. I remember we were listening to the Green Day song,

"Good Riddance." Out of the blue, my dad screamed my name. He thought I was drifting too far to the side of the road where there was a ditch.

Hearing my name screamed that loud scared me into thinking there was a deer that I didn't see so I swerved, then I overcorrected, and then I hit the ditch, and we were launched into the air.

As soon as we were airborne, the scene was quite literally like it often is portrayed in the movies—everything goes into full-on slow motion. I remember watching this unfold before my eyes while the chorus from Green Day's "Good Riddance" played.

We landed on the hood of the car and rolled three or four times. We took down four small trees. My head broke through the side window, and then I jerked forward, and my hand broke the windshield. We landed upside down, so we were only being held in by our seatbelts. There was blood all over me.

My first thought was, *Oh my god, I killed my dad.*

I turned to him and said, "Are you okay?"

He said, "Yes, are you okay?"

I said, "I think so."

I looked down then continued, "There's a lot of blood, but I don't feel any pain."

I didn't feel the gash in my hand. I didn't feel any of my body, to be honest. I climbed out of the car through the broken window. I noticed a car had stopped behind us—funnily enough, it was the high school basketball coach whose team I had tried out for when I hurt my ankle. He had pulled over to see if we were okay. There were a bunch of people who stopped to make sure we were alive and to get us help.

The coach said, "Let me call an ambulance."

I said, "No, no. I don't want an ambulance," because I didn't want Kenny to find out and call me dramatic.

A woman's voice came through the crowd, "Honey, you've got blood all over you."

I said, "I'm fine. It's just my hand. I hit my head, but there's no blood. It's just my hand. I'm fine, I'm fine. Everything is fine."

I wasn't fine, but adrenaline was flooding my brain and body convincing me that I was. I metaphorically bolted in the opposite direction in terms of getting attention for my injuries.

The first thing I thought after seeing all the blood on me was, *This is a good opportunity to show Kenny I'm tough! This is a good opportunity to show him I can get through anything. That I'm resilient!*

So what do we do? We get a fucking taxi to Thanksgiving dinner. We go straight there. I'm covered in blood. I remember I was wearing a blue Abercrombie & Fitch windbreaker with red trim, and I went into the church proudly, wearing this wind breaker as my proof that they were wrong—I wasn't dramatic.

At the end of the night, I went back to Chrysalis and my dad went back to his hotel. The next morning during breakfast, he told me that when he took off his shoes and pants that night back in his room, shards of glass tumbled out of them.

It was really a horrible accident. The van was completely totaled and if you looked at the back seat, it was completely crushed. It appeared as though there was a steel cage around my dad and me. If my mother and brother had been able to come, they would have been in the back seat, and this story would've ended much differently.

I never got medical attention for the accident. I likely had a concussion judging from the constant headaches and mood changes, which lasted several weeks. My hand healed slowly over the next three to four months. Then, one day, it randomly started to hurt again. To relieve the pain, I would massage the keloid scar that had formed.

I mostly did the massaging in Circle, as it was a way to distract myself. I'll never forget that for about three straight weeks, every time I massaged the scar in Circle, I would then see little shards of glass start poking through. My body was rejecting the glass that was never washed out of the wound. Those three weeks of Circle picking shards of glass from my scar were the most entertaining Circles I had while I was there.

Chapter Eight

HOLD TRUE TO
WHAT WE BELIEVE

I thought the three and a half years of journals I wrote when I was sent away were gone forever. I looked everywhere for months and couldn't find them. Then, unexpectedly, I found them in a closet under the stairs of our house. It is one of those closets where you put everything that doesn't fit anywhere else, like old electronic cables or craft supplies from a hobby you have abandoned. I recognized the oversized plastic tub that housed them all as soon as I saw it.

I probably should have paced myself better at that point. It's not like I didn't know what was in these journals. But the first day, I just sat there for six hours straight, reading, crying, and spiraling.

Since they were arranged chronologically, the first journals were from Intermountain Hospital. I never remembered much about my time there; it was all just a blur. I think it was all the inaccurate medications they had me on. I tried contacting the hospital later to get my records, but they said everything had been destroyed. That meant there were things I would never be able to know, and that always made me feel incomplete.

Now I was flooded with all of the things I forgot, like Desk Space, and writing out the Thirty-Six Thinking Errors, or Random Draw with those ten pieces of paper in the biohazard bag and how so many of the slips said "No."

It felt similar to how it does when I'm scrolling TikTok and see a video about kids' toys from the 1980s. You haven't thought about that doll or toy since that time, but now you're like, *Oh yeah, I remember the smell that toy had.* Except, instead of pleasant nostalgia, it was the feelings that came rushing back. *Oh yeah, I remember what it feels like to be that sad, depressed, unloved, and lonely. I remember what true hopelessness feels like.*

I brought one of the Intermountain journals to my husband, crying my eyes out. This journal talks about how sick I felt because I had to take the bipolar medications at noon, and they made me so tired. It literally says, "I just threw up. I feel so sick and dizzy. Uh-oh, I'm really feeling tired now ...." All of a sudden, you see my handwriting change and then it goes off the page. Even the energy of the doodle itself is so fried and confused and fucked up. It's just heartbreaking.

I wanted to reach into the journal and give my 15-year-old self a hug and tell her I loved her.

Chrysalis staff also tried to tell me that all of my records had been destroyed, but at least I remembered more from my three-year stay there.

For example, I remembered when the cohort of new girls came and they opened up the other house across the road by the lake. Those girls were called Lake House Girls while the ones who still resided in the original structure near the horse pasture were called Horse House Girls. I remembered facts like that, but I didn't remember how they used language, like "accountability" or "feedback" as part of their indoctrination—all of this self-help lingo that gets pushed at you and you have to memorize in order to be healthy and work the program.

I didn't remember how brainwashed I was until I traced the arc from the first couple of Chrysalis journals where I complain a lot—about my relationship with Kenny, my physical ailments, my homesickness, everything, really—and then I just stop. By the last journals, I have learned to hold everything in.

Some days reading these journals, I would feel fine. I might even think to myself, "Wow, okay, the worst is over now ...." only to have something trigger a new memory that would rip me back open again.

Mother Mary

At Chrysalis, you had to journal every day. However, gone were the days of using a journal to confess your deepest fears and emotions, because your journal was not private. Every week you were expected to hand in your journal.

In her role as my "therapist," Mary would read my journal every week and comment all over it in intrusive colors of ink. Her scrawls called up the worst kind of editor, redlining my thoughts, offering ways to improve myself, covering the margins with questions like, "How can you be a better person so people will like you more? How can you fit in more? What do you need to change?"

Interestingly, Mary never commented on anything that had to do with Kenny. Many times I would lay out the abuse I received from her husband. I would describe all of the ways that Kenny was cruel and how it made me sad.

"I'm really upset right now because we were at breakfast, and when I was putting syrup on my plate, I accidentally spilled some onto the placemat. Kenny called me a pig."

I complained about how Kenny didn't like me. How Kenny had his favorites and treated them so differently than he did me. How I had to try ten times as hard to get any kind of praise—praise that I wanted and needed so badly. I'd say things like, "I just want to feel loved. It's really hard not being hugged. I want to be around people I feel that like me."

Mary refused to discuss any of that. She never validated my feelings. She never said something in response like, "I understand this is so scary." In my opinion, if she valued my health and my safety, if she truly wanted me to get "better," these would be things she'd want to address.

I also described times when Kenny ignored my medical needs. In one entry I write, "We were clearing brush piles in the horse pasture today. Kenny was cutting down a tree with his chainsaw, and it was too loud to hear 'Timber!' and the tree fell and hit me right on the head. Kenny got mad at me for being in the way and didn't ask if I was okay."

On another page I wrote something like, "I had a horse-riding lesson today, but I got really scared when the horse started acting erratic, and when I yelped, the horse kicked me off. Kenny yelled at me for it."

Is it possible that Mary really believed she was truly helping us? I suppose. I cannot begin to try to understand the massive number of cognitive biases involved if she did, though. I pretty much begged her for years to help me feel more loved and told her about the abuse I was receiving, while she did nothing.

Kenny, in my opinion, was a narcissist looking for something to feed his ego. I don't think Mary was a narcissist; I hesitantly believe that Mary was also a victim. It has since been reported to me that Kenny would sometimes yell at his staff, not treat them very kindly, and at times even inaccurately paid his staff for hours worked. From where I was sitting in my viewpoint back then, and from what I have heard from staff and survivors he came into contact with, he mistreated many people around him, and I wouldn't be surprised if that included Mary.

As you can see, my feelings about Mary are very complicated. There were times when Mary made me smile, and there were even times when I felt like she cared about me. On the other hand, she also stood by and watched a lot of us be mistreated.

Mary was supposed to be my therapist, and there were a lot of things she did that I didn't think were okay. For example, she very much wanted to be seen in the role of a mother figure. One of her notes in a journal says as much explicitly, "Do you see connections between me and your mother?"

No, Mary, not really, I want to say now. *I want to see you as my therapist. Have you tried asking yourself what your needs are that are not being met in the world for you to even ask me that question?*

Another time, I must have made a joke about Mary getting a Camaro, but apparently, it really hurt her feelings. So in my journal entry, I apologize. It is the sincerest apology you can imagine coming out of a 17-year-old, written through the lens of an obvious fear of being abandoned because of it, but her response was incredibly misguided.

"I forgive you," she wrote, "but sometimes I feel like you don't see me as a person."

That is not my job, Mary, I'm thinking now. *It is not my job to placate you, my therapist, or be your emotional support. You are supposed to be mine.*

A Bounded Choice

Mary had her LCPC, which meant she was a licensed clinical professional counselor. She was also a Licensed Addiction Counselor (LAC), and she pushed the addiction angle every chance she could. It felt like anyone who had ever done a drug was an addict, and anyone who'd ever had a drink was an alcoholic in her book.

I said to her many times, "Mary, I don't think I'm an alcoholic. I mean, I'm not sitting here craving it. If I was an addict, wouldn't I be struggling with wanting to do drugs?"

Her responses were always defensive and projected straight back at me. At Chrysalis, they always wanted us to lack confidence; if you were confident you were not an addict so they would attack you there. Mary either ignored my perspective or had me think about things for so long that I began to believe her thoughts were my thoughts. And she succeeded.

I accepted that I was who they told me that I was. They had not only broken my spirit, but they also effectively molded me into a tool to be used for their own gain. I had to go to AA and NA for three years, get a sponsor, identify myself as a user whose life was unmanageable, and had to work the 12 Steps.

Before my senior year at Chrysalis, the Lake House was having some problems. If I remember correctly, there were lots of girls breaking the rules, and I think some girls were having sex. Mary and Kenny explained to me that there was no leadership there besides the house parents and told me they'd like to send me over there to live and help out by "showing my leadership skills." There I was again being forced out of a house where I had finally begun to feel settled into a routine. I know why they chose me. It is because I am so rigid with rule following, and they knew that the coercive control they had taught me could be used on the other girls.

For the record, I am using this word *leadership* very loosely. Leadership in this case simply meant they could count on me to hold people accountable and criticize them. If people were not following the rules, you called them out. That is their version of leadership. You shame them, and force change that isn't natural.

So, Chrysalis was not only grooming us to be ongoing abuse victims who never speak up, but they were also attempting to groom us to be future abusers by creating a craving for constant conflict.

It happens in cults the same way when you wake up years later, you are hit with the realization that not only were you hurt yourself, but you hurt other people because of the indoctrination you underwent.

Sociologist and world-renowned cult expert, Dr. Janja Lalich, describes in her Bounded Choice framework how a person's options become so limited and constrained. Janja (who is now a good friend) describes the four dimensions of an organization that qualifies them as a cultic system.

There is a leader who exhibits charismatic authority.

There is a transcendent belief system or overarching ideology.

There are systems of control in place, visible mechanisms that regulate the group.

Lastly, there are systems of influence at play where members learn to adapt their thoughts, attitudes, and behaviors in relation to their new beliefs.

To me, that framework really answers all the questions people are inclined to ask survivors like me.

Why didn't you run?

How did you not know this was abuse?

How could you not speak up for other people?

If you're a good person, why did you hurt other people?

The answer is that I had no choice. I was operating within the moral values of the group. My morality was the leaders' immorality. And to progress and survive, I had to adapt and conform any way I could.

Of course, that mental incarceration didn't leave me just because I graduated from Chrysalis. It remained in every fiber of my being, every choice I made.

I really wanted to be a doctor growing up but I remember being in the Suburban with Kenny and worrying about how hard it was going to be to go to college and then make it all the way through medical school.

I asked Kenny, "Do you think I'm smart enough to go to med school?"

He said, "I don't know, maybe." Which was the same thing as saying, "No." It wasn't a yes. To me, that meant it might not be a good idea, so I had to find another way to make him proud.

I wanted to achieve the best of the best. I needed to be the best of the best so that people around me would think I was okay. It's the reason I became so obsessed with grades.

Before I got sent away from my home, I was getting Bs and Cs, but in Eureka, I got all As during my junior and senior years. Why? I was trying desperately to impress Kenny.

That streak continued when I attended Carroll College in Helena, Montana. If I got a B, I was extremely upset. It was an extremely unhealthy relationship with success that I was developing. I was doing better in school, but I wasn't doing it for myself, I was doing it for acceptance, and for people to think better things about me. I was trying to control the narrative, to create one that made me more ideal and more wanted, because that wasn't what I felt like at my core.

I Went to a Boarding School

By the time I got my Level Three at Chrysalis, I was allowed to have a boyfriend. He went to Lincoln High School in Eureka. Kenny and Mary still controlled our relationship; we weren't allowed to be intimate or kiss, but we were still technically dating.

Even after graduating high school, the reason I stayed in Montana for college was probably pretty typical for a heterosexual teenage girl—I stayed because of this boy.

He chose to go to the University of Montana in Missoula which was a big state school. I wanted to follow him there, but my parents thought a small, private college would be more my speed. Then, if I showed I could handle that, they would allow me to transfer. Then, the summer before college he broke up with me. I had already enrolled in college so now I was stuck in Montana. Again.

When I first got to college, I struggled. I was thrown into this social world where I had no idea what was going on. When I thought you were supposed to do A, it turned out you were supposed to do B, C, or D—anything but A. I had to relearn the entire world while simultaneously being hampered by these fallacies that I believed about myself. I think some of my social issues had to do with being autistic, but I also had to unlearn things I learned from Chrysalis that were causing me big problems.

It was also frustrating every time someone asked me, "Where did you go to high school?" I always tried to avoid the slew of questions that would undoubtedly follow my real answer. Instead, I skirted the truth by saying, "I went to a boarding school." I had a series of canned responses that both satisfied others for a time and also helped me avoid facing what had happened to me. Every now and then my friends continued to probe, and once I explained the situation more fully, I always saw a reaction of, "Woah. What?"

I remember my new boyfriend in college saying, "That's kind of fucked up your parents did that." In my head, I rationalized everything.

He just doesn't understand what it was like.

He doesn't understand how good it was for me, and how it saved my life.

I was unlovable before Chrysalis.

Those kinds of rationalizations were implanted by Chrysalis.

If people think that Chrysalis was bad, they must not understand.

You understand Lizzy. Others might not, but you need to hold true to what you believe—and we decide what that is.

Being autistic, I always had an inability to understand social situations; I never caught on as quickly as others. Then along came Chrysalis to explain the world to me. I embraced it. It was a relief, actually, to have that level of certainty for the first time in my life.

College brought forth a lot of situations where my programming butted up against the expectations and experiences of others, and that's when I realized that the world Chrysalis explained was definitely not the real world.

For example, one friend and I had a disagreement over something she did that I didn't like. I confronted her in a very direct, Chrysalis-like fashion, which didn't work in the outside world. Instead, it drove us apart, and the friendship faltered because of the way that I acted.

Another time, I actually tried a Circle with a group of friends. Chrysalis never explained any of the evidence-based research for why they do what they do. (My guess is that it doesn't exist). It was through their careful modeling that I came to believe that all relationships require confrontation and conflict.

They never told us, "Hey, we're doing things a certain way here, but it's going to be a little different when you leave. We're trying to teach you how to stick up for yourself and that means sometimes, unfortunately, you're going to have conflict. But as you get more skilled, you'll realize when it's necessary and when it's not." They don't say things like that. They just make you think that when your friend is pissing you off, that you can get ahead by making them feel like shit. Double the points if it's in front of their peers.

Needless to say, the result of my attempted Circle was a bunch of other college-age girls sitting around saying, "What the fuck?"

Those were some of my first indicators that this is not the way the world works.

Chrysalis's hold on me was complicated by the fact that they continued to be in touch with me while I was at college. Six months into my freshman year, I got an email from Mary which read: "I have heard that you've been partying and drinking. I wanted to give you a chance to tell your side of the story. Would you like to hold yourself accountable?"

Looking back now, I think, that must have been illegal, right? I'm not their patient anymore, and I'm over 18. Did I respond with budding individuation and challenge Mary for contacting me at all, now that I was free?

I did not.

Instead, I fawned all over her. (Boy, did they still have a hold on me.) "I made such a big mistake," I wrote. "I am so sorry. Will you forgive me?"

Gross. It makes me sick just thinking about it.

There was another thing that happened freshman year that showed the extent of my indoctrination. I got an email from Mary and Kenny saying they wanted my help. They told me that because I was such a success story from Chrysalis, (flattering me into thinking I was someone special) they wanted me to tell my story to the Montana State Legislature in support of a bill.

This bill, if passed, would block regulation in the Troubled Teen Industry by standing in the way of another bill that was intended to regulate the industry.

I remember them telling me, "If our bill passes, it'll ensure that places like Chrysalis won't ever feel like a lockdown facility."

I had been to a lockdown facility, and I thought, *Well, I don't want that.*

They said, "If this doesn't pass, we're going to have to secure the knives. We're going to have to lock the doors at night and make sure everyone is held involuntarily."

Was that true? I don't know. I didn't even know what a bill was at that point. But they told me it would "institutionalize" Chrysalis. I thought *I've got to go take care of the Chrysalis family.*

I also thought, *Oh my gosh, are they going to accept me now? Maybe I'll be one of the girls that Kenny really likes after this.*

So, Mary and Kenny drove down to Helena, Montana with a white van full of Chrysalis girls and everyone testified.

It is horrifying and embarrassing now to think of myself sitting in a room being part of an effort which successfully blocked regulations of Montana programs. But, it also illustrates how much damage they had done, how indoctrinated I was, and how I believed everything they told me.

I want to add one P.S. here. My senior year in college, I was set to graduate with honors in my chosen major of psychology. At the time, I thought I chose that field because I wanted to learn about how people think. Now that I have connected the dots regarding my neurodivergence, I am sure that some of my motivation was that the more I studied people and behavior, the more normal I could pretend to be. Furthermore, I think that, subconsciously, I was trying to figure out what happened to me in the hospital and at Chrysalis and why. I was searching for answers.

The full indoctrination I received unfortunately affected even my employment choices while in college. In order to fulfill the requirements for my major, I had to do a practicum for two semesters in some kind of mental healthcare environment. In Helena, Montana, there aren't many options for this, but I knew I wanted to work with children in some way, so I ended up working at what I thought was a children's hospital.

It turned out to be a TTI facility.

It was located in Helena, Montana, and it housed children from the ages of 3 to 18. I didn't have any kind of real access—all I really did was the charts in the teen unit—but I saw the staff there regulate every single second of the kids' days. We were forced to watch them like a hawk; they tell you that it's for their own good. I followed directions, and I believed them.

I erroneously thought that the word "hospital" meant that it existed to help kids. While some people may not have considered this hospital a TTI program then, I definitely do now. I am sure I am not alone in that, as reports have recently flooded the media about children escaping, and some dying trying to escape, while others have committed suicide inside the hospital's walls.

I saw kids on safety. I saw kids being restrained. Why didn't it connect for me that I had seen those situations—even been subjected to them—in Boise, Idaho? How could I never question the way this experience was replicating a past that lay buried in bad feelings for me?

I have no idea how I missed the red flags. Maybe it was because this all fell under the umbrella of "psychology." *This is an experience I am having where I will learn about abnormal psychology. This is off a list that Carroll College gave me of approved practicums, so this is okay.* It could have been any number of rationalizations, but it truly showed the cognitive dissonance that's possible when you've been brainwashed.

Chapter Nine

A REPEAT
SPONGE OFFENDER

After graduating from college, I moved into the nonprofit space to work. By the time I was 24, I was the vice president and managing director at the Gochnauer Foundation and on three separate non-profit boards, monitoring investments, generating media interest including my own public speaking and helping to define the missions of these respective organizations.

The one thing I did correctly in my life without fail was advancing my professional career. I somehow managed to keep my professional career and reputation completely unblemished.

Meanwhile my personal life was always crumbling into pieces.

My formative years in the TTI groomed me into believing I did not deserve to be treated well, not only in the world of friendships but also in the area of love relationships.

I think that is something people don't always realize about the abuse happening in TTI facilities. It's not only what happened back then that's not okay. It's also about how those toxic behaviors become normalized for survivors, and then repeat endlessly until survivors find a combination of strength, luck, and knowledge to break the cycle.

For example, I felt like I was molded in the TTI to become the perfect future domestic abuse victim. When I experienced domestic violence in my first two marriages, it reiterated the narrative in my head that I was bad. I was the issue. I was the problem. That's what they taught us, and it is absolutely what my ex-husbands said as well.

Subconsciously, Kenny had become the image of who I wanted to be with. It makes me feel so sick to admit that now, but our interactions became the model of what I thought I deserved and should subsequently look for in how I'm treated by a spouse. I didn't see the way he treated me as abuse. I saw it as what a relationship was supposed to be.

So when my one ex husband's narcissistic rage would bubble to the surface and he started treating me like I don't matter, I would think to myself, *Well, that's what people do. Kenny used to do that too.* I was thoroughly indoctrinated into believing that if something bad happened to me, I deserved it.

The personal accountability that was drilled into me really amounted to everything being my fault. *If he's abusing me, what did I do to cause it, and how do I fix it?* That in turn conditioned me to do whatever was going to make men happy with me.

I became chronically attracted to guys that made me work for it. *Are they going to love me or not?* That was a question that kept me on the edge of my seat.

Just as Kenny would approve of me one day, and then I'd have to gain his approval the next, in my dating and married life I went after guys that treated me poorly; guys that were less available. I never knew if I was going to wake up with someone that loved me or not. It created a kind of dopamine rush when the guy did want me, like, *Yes! I've got him. I've got him.* But that intermittent gratification doesn't last in the long run.

When you go out looking for someone who will treat you well, then push you away—when that is your type—you can find them. It was even better if they were the kind of guy that I thought I could never get.

In short, narcissists loved me. They loved the fact that I would exhibit the personality of whoever I was around. I was a social chameleon. I enjoyed being social, but three-and-a-half years of being told that I was socially inept inhibited me from revealing my own social personality at first. My special interest of people watching led to my greatest defense mechanism—becoming an expert adapter and sponge of other people's personalities.

I have learned that this is relatively common in autistic individuals, and taking on the personality of those they are around becomes a protective measure against being criticized or perceived as socially "off." If you act like the person you are talking to, how could they be annoyed? I used to laugh to myself when people would compliment me.

"You have such a great personality!" they'd say.

"Hahaha thanks … it's YOURS!" I'd say in response.

I was a repeat sponge offender, and it is still part of my therapy to learn how to take off that mask and be okay with who I am.

A Catalogue of Abusive Relationships

I could create an entire catalogue of narcissistic abuse that I suffered after leaving Chrysalis, until I met my now-husband, Ben. I have endured gaslighting that far outdid what I felt Kenny and Mary inflicted upon me. Men would abuse me in some way, shape, or form and then follow it up with, "If you weren't so [fill in the blank] then I wouldn't have to do this to you!"

I've had to detect fake accents and hidden addictions.

I have filed restraining orders.

I have broken said restraining orders when I missed them again.

I've heard words that sound caring but are so loaded like,

"Man, it must be hard to feel so unwanted. Your parents sent you away. I can't imagine the kind of abandonment that you must feel knowing that no one wants you."

One time, when my ex-husband found out I called my Dad for advice before him, he told me, "If you respect your dad so much, why don't you just go fuck him?"

That same husband would insult my family behind their backs in an effort to place a wedge in our relationships. For instance, he would refer to my gay brother as a "faggot."

I look back now and think, *How could I have stayed with him for as long as I did?* At the same time, there is a question that is just as real, *How could I have thought that this was not only a completely normal response but that I deserved it?*

I've dealt with a hair-trigger temper paired with the scariest eyes that I've ever seen in my life.

I've looked into the eyes of someone I was married to and seen nothing, like the absence of a soul.

I've been choked, thrown around, and shoved down.

I've had things thrown at me and my children.

I've endured verbal abuse for being an inconvenient patient when I was recovering from childbirth-related surgery.

I've been screamed at in the middle of the night, "Would you shut the fucking kid up already?!" while crying and attempting to get my newborn son to latch on while breastfeeding when the poor boy was starving.

I've seen my spouse beat up their dog (fortunately, the dog lived).

I told a husband I was thinking of leaving him, and he put his head down between his legs and started to cry. But when he looked up to see if I was watching, I noticed that there were no tears to match his crying noises.

I've left because of abuse, then I've gone back—only to then leave again.

I lacked the solid foundation of self-esteem and self-trust to make good on my escape.

I've suffered self doubt, and then rationalized and re-narrated the abuse in my head.

Maybe I was too hard on him.

Maybe it was the hormones from pregnancy that made me act like that, like he said.

Maybe he is right, and he is the best I'll ever be able to get.

Maybe he is right, no other guy will take a single mom like me.

I really hope I didn't just give up on something too easily.

Oh my god, I did. I gave up too easy. I do love him.

Later on I learned that the trauma bond we create with an abuser is a twisted dance between experiencing mistreatment and occasional kindness from an abuser. It creates a deep emotional tie that complicates the already challenging task of breaking free from an abusive relationship.

Trauma bonding, and the cycle it creates, is something I experienced to a great degree with Kenny and Mary, and with my subsequent abusive relationships as well.

When trying to explain to people what this looks like, I like to use this analogy.

Let's pretend you were bitten by a black widow spider. What would you do? I'd venture to say that most people's instincts would be to immediately go and find a doctor to administer anti-venom, right?

Now imagine that, instead of finding medical help for that poison, you spend your precious time trying to catch the black widow so you can ask it why it bit you and prove to it that you didn't deserve that bite.

That is trauma bonding.

In my life, this has been one of the most chaotic, toxic, and hardest things to get out of. Furthermore, staying in relationships like that can oftentimes affect more than just you, especially if there are children involved that can get bit too.

I like to think that I have never been one to look back on my past with regrets. In fact, I have two Spanish phrases tattooed on my wrists. "Sín Lamentos," which means "No Regrets," is on my left wrist and "Porqué no," which means "Why not," is on my right one. These both highlight my view of taking every opportunity that arises and, if things ever don't work out, to not look backwards with regret.

Despite that, I do have what I would consider one regret. That regret is that my decisions started Spencer and Jackson's lives off in such a traumatic way. They had to deal with the trauma of having a biological father who was virtually non-existent as they grew up. When they were about six and eight years old, their long-absent dad randomly took me to court to fight to have visitation, so I granted that (against my intuition that it wouldn't turn out well).

After six months of finally building a relationship with Spencer and Jackson every other weekend, he called me on my birthday and told me he "wanted out" of being a parent. He told me he wanted to give up his rights to the kids and wanted me to make sure that they didn't contact him.

They never got to say goodbye.

At first, the kids blamed me for his decision. Believe it or not, I was okay with that, I almost expected that, as I am the "safe" parent. I accepted that blame and let them put that on me because I don't think they felt comfortable putting it anywhere else.

When we as parents look at our kids who are in pain and say, "I wish I could take the pain away from you!," this was my version of that. This was my way of trying to soak up all their pain so they could be mad at someone who was safe and would never leave them.

The healing that the children have had to do from this has been extensive and ongoing. I know a piece of that trauma from being adopted at birth and feeling abandoned in my teenage years, but this was at a whole new level. He straight out abandoned his young children. How do you explain to children that this has nothing to do with them? How do you explain narcissism?

I feel so lucky that my children took after me, instead of their father, and have deep compassion, love, and empathy; but how do I make sure they know they're nothing like him?

Spencer and Jackson are two of the most resilient children I have ever known. I obviously love all my children and have different types of bonds with them all, but Spencer, Jackson, and I went through extremely difficult, traumatic, and abusive times together before little Harper and Bentley arrived. This gave us a bond that is very tight knit. We have our matching battle scars, but I purposefully attempted to transform those scars into a bond and something we can share and grow from to ensure that the three of us don't feel separated from each other because of it but feel a link from our shared experience.

Your Eyes Tell a Story

After I was divorced for the second time, I went through a long period of being really heartbroken. I had to accept that I might not find anyone else and that that was okay. I think calling a pause really allowed me to mature and become the person I needed to be in order to find the person I'm supposed to be with.

I know other survivors who have encountered this paradox—finding peace within yourself, outside of a relationship, allows you to find a better relationship. This calling a pause, or being given a pause, is important so you don't just go from abusive indoctrination to abusive relationship to abusive relationship to abusive relationship.

How are you supposed to find someone who's perfect for you if you don't know who you are?

The pause allowed me to learn slowly what a man should act like. I was being deprogrammed from trying to find a young Kenny.

Fortunately for me, I ran into Gigi. Gigi looks the exact opposite of me. She's blonde, with a big bust and a tiny waist. She has porcelain skin and big hair. But deep down, we're the same—our sense of humor, our depth. She became my best friend.

Having said that, it was a full year into our friendship before we had a conversation about our childhoods.

"Where did you go to high school?" I asked.

She said, "I went to boarding school."

I thought, *Hmmm. That sounds like something I have said many times myself.* "I went to boarding school, too," I replied. "Where did you go?"

"Montana."

"What? Where?"

"Spring Creek Lodge."

Spring Creek Lodge was a pretty horrific place.

That's when it hit me: We were in Montana, in TTI programs, at the same time.

We were both survivors.

Because Gigi is neurotypical she was able to teach me about red flags in relationships.

I'm a very genuine person. What you see is what you get with me. Because of that authenticity, I sometimes miss the games that need to be played. She taught me about why it's important to play those games even if you're not a game player.

For example, when I was single again and got a text from some guy, she would read it and say, "That's not okay." Or she'd say, "I know that you're excited about that text but you're going to wait an hour before you respond." Gigi taught me how to not come off too needy in the beginning.

Now I was back to embracing men who were more like my father. I view my father as incredibly humble, and it is amazing the way he treats my mom. The guys that didn't like my dad, didn't like him because they felt threatened by him. And, truth be told, my dad didn't really care for my first two husbands either. It wasn't until he met Ben that he said to my Mom privately, "Wow, I don't have to worry about Meg being taken care of anymore."

On February 27, 2018, I saw Ben on Tinder and I swiped right.

I had just recently adjusted my settings on the app. I was not finding anyone who was worth my time, so where I previously had a radius of 25 miles in which to locate potential matches, I now expanded that range to 60 miles.

With the increased range I started to see new people on the app, and one of them was Ben. I remember thinking, *Man, I'm sure he's not going to swipe right on me.* That might have been the low self-esteem talking.

I had also been fully transparent in my bio; by that point, I had three kids. I had heard of single parents who don't tell you they have children until you meet. I think that's a waste of time to potentially spend time investing into a connection, only to find out they won't date a single mom. I didn't want to date anyone unless they already knew what they were signing up for. (Chaos. They were signing up for chaos.)

Nothing happened when I swiped right, meaning I was the first to do so. The next morning when I woke up, however, the app read, "You have new matches." Ben was one of those matches. I thought to myself, *Whaaat? Damn, awesome.*

I sent Ben a message that said, "You seriously have the best smile. There's nothing better than a great smile." That was my first message to him.

I found out later that he had recently changed his radius to 60 miles as well. Then, I realized we lived exactly 60 miles apart. If we had been 61 miles apart, we wouldn't have matched.

We gelled immediately. I knew he was the one before I even physically met him. After a little more than a week of knowing him, I wrote a poem about him:

Your eyes tell a story
Your soul is the plot
Reading the book that is you
Rids my tender heart's knot

Passion oozing from your words
Yearning to draw you in close
Hold my hand, touch my heart
Be my overdose

Electrify my energy
purify my poisoned heart
You're the answer to everything
You're my restart

I felt safe enough to have him come pick me up at my house for our first date. Normally, I like having an escape. I like having my own car. (That's something that I've heard many survivors tell me they can relate to, having been held against their will for any length of time.)

Things were feeling very natural to him as well. He asked me before we ever met, "What are you doing on March 14th?" I wasn't sure whether to play it cool, as Gigi was suggesting, or play it straight. I chose the latter.

"Nothing," I said.

"My mom's coming to town," he told me.

"Are you asking me to meet your mom before we've even met?" I asked.

Since his mom was going to be visiting from Iowa, we made plans to take her to see a live show by talk-show personality Conan O'Brien while she was in town.

In the meantime, we had our first date—just the two of us. We went to the Rooftop Lounge in Laguna Beach and I felt extremely comfortable with him, like I had known him my entire life. Afterwards he came back to the house with me and met the kids. We had a dance party. That never happened. I don't let people meet my kids that fast.

He was a server in San Diego so he worked nights. He would come visit us late every Saturday night after his shift ended and then stay with us for his two days off, Sunday and Monday. We'd hang out with the kids and do fun things.

He very quickly, and effortlessly, became part of the family.

The Trauma Spiral of 2018

Just because we were connected and meant to be, didn't mean we didn't have our challenges.

For one thing, I represented the end of Ben's bachelor life. As wonderful as our times were together, he could still escape back to San Diego.

He later told me that he really struggled within himself. He wanted to be alone, but he also wanted me. And so we went, back and forth, and it was pretty intense.

I didn't know it at the time, but he was battling undisclosed addiction issues. And on my side, I had already been dealing with massive panic attacks for about a year. I was not able to go out in public unless I took a Xanax ahead of time because I knew I would be having a panic attack and by then it would be too late. So I was pre-treating my panic attacks.

Ben and I went on our first cruise together in August of 2018 for our 6 months anniversary and it was a disaster. My anxiety and panic attacks mixed with his addiction struggles led to a very toxic trip.

After returning home from the cruise, I didn't feel as anxious, so I stopped taking Xanax altogether. Then coincidentally, Ben broke up with me that same day. Something terrible happened inside me during what would turn out to be a perfect storm of hurt.

I knew intuitively that I was going to marry Ben, but now it was like my path had been altered. There was a glitch in the matrix. It was that kind of feeling, *I'm not real. Is this real?*

What started then was a severe two-week period of depersonalization, derealization, and dissociation.

As most people who are panicking do, I frantically searched for answers as to why I felt like this. *Could all of this be withdrawal from a mild dose of Xanax?* I latched on to that theory since it made some sense of things. I was in a full panic for two weeks straight; for 24 hours a day. When the kids weren't in school and daycare, I had no choice but to have a nanny there with me. Having another adult there made me feel better, because I was so scared that at any point I would drop dead and leave my kids without anyone to take care of them.

I think what happened was by that point Ben had become a crutch. He was my safe place, and then he left.

I wrote another poem, a darker one this time, more like a journal entry from the old days, to remind myself about how I was feeling in case I ever became anxious enough to think I needed to take Xanax again.

"Today was the worst day of my life. Far beyond any of the abuse I've experienced in my life was what I felt today …. Withdrawals from Xanax.

Every single fiber in my body was tingling as if it had scorching hot water slowly being poured on it, but it was odd-ly so cold that I was shivering. My mind became a black hole of emptiness and evil, open to bombarding negative thoughts as if demons now had a hold of it. My soul felt as empty as it has ever been and I felt myself solely relying on those around me to remind me of who I was, what I was capable of, and that I wasn't going to die like I thought I was.

For most, this is similar to what they've experienced as a panic attack but it lasted every single moment of the day and nothing could hold it back or push it forward. It was stuck in the middle of 'panic' and 'not panic' and my mind was stuck begging for it to either move forward so I could panic and get it over with or begging for it to just go away. It came as nu-merous tsunamis plowing through my soul tempting to wash me away but only pushing me a tiny bit closer to death while I was begging for it to just take me away for good."

I was stuck.

I was miserable.

I was completely and utterly obliterated from the inside out.

Forget being abducted in the middle of the night. I had never felt so much fear and anguish in my entire life. I would endure the TTI ten times over again to never feel what I felt in those two weeks.

I didn't know what to do, so I did what any child—which is what I felt like at the time—would do.

I called my parents.

I was crying my eyes out. I said, "I think something's wrong. I don't know what it is. I feel like I'm going crazy. I'm so scared. I can't leave the room. I can't breathe, I can't speak. Help me."

My dad immediately got on a plane and came out to stay with me for two weeks. My psychiatrist had me take Benadryl around the clock to calm me down enough that I wouldn't go into a full-blown panic attack.

I kept thinking, *I don't know what to do. I'm going to die. I'm going to die. I'm going to die.*

The psychiatrist I had at the time confirmed this wasn't withdrawal, as I had been on way too low a dose to be experiencing symptoms this severe. So what was it?

Years later, after waking up, she confirmed It was likely Complex Post-Traumatic Stress Disorder (CPTSD) coming to the tipping point to where it could not be ignored any longer.

It was a full-on trauma spiral of CPTSD, likely compounded by an autistic shutdown.

It was everything from the TTI, from being abducted, from all of the trauma, from Kenny, Mary, my low self-esteem, abandonment, and all the abuse I had in the subsequent abusive marriages.

Everyone in my life now colloquially refers to this time as the Trauma Spiral of 2018.

I look back at this time as absolutely the worst time of my life.

For those two weeks, I couldn't leave the house without someone with me, and I couldn't be alone in my house without another adult. I felt so lucky to have a Dad who dropped everything to be there to both help me and the kids during this time.

I was so petrified from the way my brain felt that I was going to go crazy, have psychosis of some sort, and then die leaving my children alone in this world. My greatest fear. But I eventually managed to get through to the other side.

As the storm within me subsided, I emerged with newfound resilience, determined to reclaim my life from the shadows of despair and forge a path toward healing and hope.

Chapter Ten

IT'S TIME TO WAKE UP

B en reached back out to me after two weeks, right around when the worst of my trauma spiral was ending. While I was feeling a little bit more stable from the spiral, I know part of the reason I ended up taking him back was because I still relied on him so much as a crutch. If he was around, I didn't have to be alone. He felt safe because he grounded me. Being alone was scary, and the thoughts that came up from suppressing trauma were horrific. I had no idea that this was related to my time in the TTI, but it did start me on the road to waking up about my experience.

The next six months were hell on my mental health. I did everything in my power to figure out how to get the therapy I needed, although I still didn't know what was wrong with me.

Ben and I were back together at this point, but he was struggling internally and I had no idea. He had confessed to being an alcoholic shortly before my trauma spiral, and his first day of sobriety coincided with my trauma spiral.

I started my healing journey by focusing on a healthy body. I started working out every day and eating very clean foods, believing that energy and nutrition would fuel positive mental health benefits.

Ben continued to break up with me every month or so, and without warning, over and over again. However, each breakup that occurred almost chipped away at that crutch I used him for. With every breakup, I became more capable and independent, and loved myself more. I was becoming proud of who I was. I was beginning to understand, and appreciate, my worth.

It happened gradually, but I began to notice I wasn't as scared to leave the house or be alone. I would notice that where I would've normally had a panic attack, I wasn't anymore. I started to feel independent, strong, capable and my self-worth was developing rapidly.

Finally Finding Home

The last time Ben broke up with me, I remember feeling so fed up, instead of being sad. It was over absolutely nothing, as always. He went to bed the night before telling me how much he loved me, then woke up the next morning with the opposite to say.

I think he was surprised because this time, I didn't cry. This time I said, "Well okay, that is your decision."

I decided I deserved better, so I let him walk off, get in his car, and drive back to San Diego. This time I didn't text him at all.

When he reached out to mend things with me two weeks later, I felt a stronger sense of myself than I ever had before.

"I'm sorry," I told him, "I'm dating people. I'm moving on. This is not what I deserve in a relationship."

It was true. I had been on one date. But I also knew Ben was the one. Maybe I had finally understood what Gigi had been teaching me. So I told him, "I'm not going to date you unless you agree to go to therapy."

He agreed. I was learning boundaries and respect.

That prompted our first therapy appointment. In that session, Ben confessed that despite having been clean from alcohol for six months, he had been struggling with active drug addiction. The breakups were simply him attempting to escape and find solitude where he could make unhealthy decisions.

This therapy session was the beginning of learning how to communicate better and rebuild trust. We spent time processing the relationships within our extended family and how they affected us and unpacking the breakups that had plagued our relationship.

We both came to the point where we realized that getting through this would make us so much stronger and so much more connected. I also realized that people who try to control others in a relationship by withholding love do not deserve to be in your life, and I made it clear to Ben that I wouldn't accept that in the future.

To Ben's credit, he was showing he was open to therapy, he was open to self-help, he was open to healing parts of himself. We were both open to change and growth.

We placed little plaques around the house that say, "You are my home." We always joked about that. Our song is called "Home" by Lack of Afro because he always felt like home. I am willing to put in the work, because with Ben I am finally home.

So we worked hard, mended our relationship, and on October 19th, 2018, we got married. At our wedding, I read aloud that poem I'd written to him in our very first week of meeting.

In my eyes, addiction and trauma are similar in that they are both something that you will inevitably deal with for the rest of your lives. They don't disappear with therapy, and even those who receive intense treatment will likely still experience highs and lows throughout their lives because of the way they both function.

I think it took a while for me to realize that something like a marriage doesn't take away those hardships. It is not the end of challenges, rather it is the beginning of a long road with many ups and downs.

Just because Ben and I were married didn't mean we were done growing. In fact we both had no idea just how long our healing journey, both individually and as a couple, would be.

Ben and I have always "meshed" for lack of a better term. He is so similar to me, but also so different. We are both extremely goofy, and always prioritize humor in our relationship. In fact, one of our all-time favorite sayings (we even have a plaque with this) is, "Marriage: An endless sleepover with your favorite weirdo." That really summed up the beginning of our marriage.

Four months after our wedding, and after going through IVF to conceive Bentley, the entire world suddenly shut down due to Covid-19.

There we were as newlyweds, freshly pregnant with our first child together. Ben was now a stay-at-home Dad, and we were homeschooling our three children. It was chaos, and it was also scary. Because of my other health issues, I was very high risk of having complications if I became infected with Covid-19. Plus I was pregnant and we didn't know what Covid-19 might do to the fetus.

We were locked down completely to protect our family.

The only way that I found comfort during my alone time was watching movies, TV shows, and documentaries to escape my thoughts and worries. Then, a few months before Bentley was born, I came across "This is Paris" on YouTube and watched it.

I had no idea what kind of journey that documentary was going to embark me on, but it opened up the gates to my trauma. In what felt like five seconds, hundreds of adolescent memories had been re-narrated and recategorized as abuse. I was waking up.

Poor Ben sat there looking at me wide-eyed and horrified as I gasped for air while crying incessantly. He came over to me to try and comfort me by placing his hand on me. "Do … do you want a hug?" he said.

"No! No hug! Need space!" I remember screaming back, fueled by some sort of autopilot system in my body rather than my own desires. I realized that I wasn't ready for any touch, and all I could do was tell Ben to give me that space.

I could barely find words, I was completely dissociated, and the trauma had taken over.

That's all you can really do when this happens; ride it out. I had to let my brain have the space it needed to adjust to its new reality. Through the years of denying my trauma, I had slowly distanced myself from my memories; unknowingly, this also cut the tether to my emotions, one by one. I had learned to intellectualize all of my emotions to better keep me from feeling anything triggering.

This is not something unique. In fact, I suspect that most survivors who left their program with any level of brainwashing know exactly how this feels; it is one of the most difficult things to go through.

The next few months were filled with eye-opening experiences that led to one of the most beneficial things I ever did for myself, which was seeking help for my trauma through EMDR Therapy. I knew I needed help because I noticed this extreme disconnect between my brain and my body. I would be sitting there calmly and all of a sudden my body would react as though something traumatic was happening in that moment. I would be doing something innocuous like watching a movie when all of a sudden I'd get sweaty, my heart would race, I'd dissociate, become irritable, and feel like I needed to flee. However, my brain wasn't feeling any fear or emotions that would make my body feel that way. It was like my body was reacting to something that my brain was unaware of. There was a disconnect.

My first stage of waking up had begun.

I'm On My Way!

After being so scared of feeling that disconnect, I decided to go all in to EMDR therapy, and found an incredible therapist named Kelly Burris. Over the next six months, I did about four hours of EMDR every week. I was determined to rid my body of this trauma and heal myself. I knew at this time I wanted to be involved in some kind of activism as well, and I knew I wouldn't be effective in that work if I hadn't deeply worked on my trauma and triggers. It was the best thing I ever did and helped me immensely.

However, while I was preoccupied on my self-help journey of healing, unbeknownst to me, Ben was quietly suffering and in the throes of addiction again, and it was coming to a tipping point. You seeing a pattern here?

After asking him about my suspicion of his substance use, he came clean to me about the past year of using without my knowing. We decided it was best for him to go to an inpatient rehab. We researched and found the one we thought would be the best one, and even talked to a consultant who had "inside knowledge" on the best programs.

The first 14 days went very smoothly, but at that point we both decided it would be best to transfer into a PHP (Partial Hospitalization Program) that would allow him to live at home because we had Bentley who was eight months old at home and being away from him was actually detrimental to Ben's recovery.

The day that Ben decided he'd let the rehab know his plans to transfer, I waited at home for a call from him to let me know how it went. Our nanny from many years before, a woman named Marcela, was on her way to our house to watch Bentley who was at home with me.

While Bentley was napping I got a call from an unknown number and answered it. It was Ben, and he was crying. His voice was shaking, and I could hear voices close to him in the background that I knew indicated his call was being monitored. I instantly knew something was wrong.

"What's wrong?" I said before he could even utter a word.

"I ... I think I'm being abused ...." he muttered through tears and obvious fear.

"Are they monitoring your call right now?"

"Yes ... they won't let me leave, and they are very angry and gaslighting me."

Something inside me shifted. I became a different person and was taken back to when I was young and being abused.

My husband was in a residential facility.

His call was being monitored.

He felt a loss of free will.

And he was being abused.

The only difference between what he went through, and what I went through was that he made the phone call asking for help that I never got to make.

In that moment, I felt a transformation into the person I am now; I became the person I needed to rescue me when I was in the programs.

"Everything is going to be okay," I told him. "Don't listen to anything they are telling you. You are an adult and can leave anytime you want. Go pack your things. I'm on my way."

When Ben stuck up for himself to the director who was angry, he told him he was never angry and if he was feeling that, perhaps that is even more of a sign that he still very much needs help. Once he announced he was leaving, he noticed that every person he had bonded with during his stay was now not even looking him in the eye. They had been instructed that Ben was now not safe to them and to not communicate with him. He had been exiled.

Meanwhile, Bentley was sleeping. I couldn't leave because Marcela hadn't arrived yet, but I couldn't wait either. So I scooped Bentley up and put him in the car. I didn't want Bentley to come with me to pick him up because I had no idea what kind of scene would go down there. Marcela met me on the side of the highway and I transferred Bentley into her car so they could go back home, and I sped off.

That 30-minute drive to the facility was filled with every emotion you could imagine — fear, dread, anger, pain, clarity, sadness, guilt, but mostly purpose. I knew that I was not only doing what I needed someone to do for me when I was young, but I was also on the path to the last stage of waking up which led to determining my purpose in this life.

When I finally arrived, Ben was already sitting outside with all of this stuff in tow. When Ben had asked them to have his records transferred to another facility that would be outpatient, the director got very angry with him and refused to do that. They even were so bold as to suggest they were "sure his wife had something to do with this decision," and had banned both him and me from the building. I have no idea why, but maybe it's because they knew I wouldn't stand for that kind of shit.

That day was the turning over of a new leaf in my life because it was the day I knew I was a survivor. It's the day I transformed myself into the person I needed and wanted to save me from my program.

Chapter Eleven
A SURVIVOR IN REAL TIME

The first survivor-based Facebook group I joined was called Breaking Code Silence (now For Survivors, By Survivors. The TTI Survivor Community).

The term "Breaking Code Silence" comes from a punishment that many programs have that takes away your ability to speak, until they see fit, called "Code Silence." #BreakingCodeSilence was the movement that was born out of that, thanks in large part to Paris Hilton's documentary which spread that impact. I found the group via Google, which is how so many good things come to us. It was during my "waking up" period that happened after watching *This is Paris*.

First, I typed in *Chrysalis survivors*, but it was hard to find any groups about my specific program. I ended up, as most survivors do when first waking up, going down a deep rabbit hole to uncover everything I could.

I remember thinking, *This industry is fucked. This entire industry is really messed up.* I could feel myself being drawn to a higher calling to join the fight to stop all this abuse.

I came across a nonprofit called Breaking Code Silence. It had been named after the hashtag and earlier movement of the same name, and I got in touch with them to see if I could use my nonprofit expertise to help them. After the first meeting I attended, I ran out to Ben in the living room and said excitedly, "I just found my people!"

It wasn't any one particular individual I was putting up on a pedestal; my experience in the TTI and subsequent healings had convinced me not to do that too quickly. It was because for the first time in my life, by connecting with members of the survivor community, I finally felt able to be myself. They knew what I was going through.

Shortly after this initial call I became the Director of Development at Breaking Code Silence, which at the time had pretty much positioned itself as being the "leader of the survivor community."

The sheer experience of speaking out for the first time against the TTI was a significant inflection point in my life. I cared so much about this movement and doing the right thing. At the same time, I was stepping into something very new. While my career in non-profits, fundraising, and board work was something I was confident in, I wasn't yet confident in this line of work. Deep down, I didn't know if I was capable of success because of all the years that I was told I wasn't.

What are we told to do when experiencing imposter syndrome? Instead of worrying about being misunderstood or feeling that I didn't belong, I turned my attention to advocacy work, and began to live and breathe the impact. Focusing on how passionate I was for the cause was the key for me.

Where there is passion, there is no anxiety.

Where there is passion, there is impact.

Where there is passion, and this was particularly important in my case, there is no mask. I am my authentic self.

And that passion turned into purpose.

I think you can work for an organization you believe in without having to make an absolute commitment to its mission. I think people do that all the time, and still do good work for society. But when your work is deeply rooted in lived experience, when your approach is based on the morals and values of having survived something, that takes it to an entirely different level.

My passion is the reason why I am so persuasive when I speak. I have been told that people are drawn to me; it isn't me, they are drawn to, however. It is the mission.

Let's say I give a keynote speech at a conference. If I get up on stage and trip over my words while I'm telling my story, that's okay, because I am a survivor. I'm talking about trauma and everyone in the audience knows that. It's not going to bother them that I am a little nervous.

For 33 years, I had to pretend like I wasn't a survivor. Then I discovered my purpose, and the healing truly began. I stopped believing that I am worth nothing. I stopped believing that I can't do anything with my life. I stopped believing that people won't like me for who I am.

It was a long road—and I am still on it. But I have everything in my power. Who knew that it was actually me that was standing in my own way.

Breaking Code Silence

I am thankful for my ability to isolate any personal struggles and keep them from affecting my professional life because I have been fortunate to have been led, mentored, and taught by some of the greatest business-minded individuals I know, and part of that education involved spending the last 20 years learning the ethical guidelines and principles that surround boards, fundraising, development, and the overall nonprofit space.

My time as director of development at Breaking Code Silence turned out to be short-lived but it was illuminating. While it showed me my purpose and I loved the mission as well as most of the incredible advocates who worked hard for the organization, I also saw things I didn't agree with. These observations forced me to be confronted with one of the most challenging decisions of my life.

As I said before, I am highly compassionate and empathetic, I see the best in people, and I somehow always naively believe that others are going to be as forthright as I am. By early December of 2021, however, I realized I could either continue to fly under the radar and not create "drama," as I had been groomed to do as a "good Chrysalis girl," or I could speak up about the issues I saw and had been professionally taught to identify and rectify.

To speak up meant it would likely hurt the first people who accepted me into the survivor community. I chose, nonetheless, to break that cycle of staying silent out of fear of not being accepted. I put the community of survivors before my own needs of feeling accepted.

At the time I spoke with the Director of Policy at Breaking Code Silence (and the eventual co-founder of Unsilenced with me). We collaborated together to try to help solve the issues we saw, but were met with refusal, so we decided it was time to move on to do the work elsewhere.

And so, on December 12th, 2021, we left to start Unsilenced.

I learned a lot at Breaking Code Silence, and it also led me to some of my best friends and a community I value beyond words— the community of survivors. It also illuminated for me why I wanted to found my own organization.

Now, We are Unsilenced

What made the name Breaking Code Silence so appealing for the beginning of the movement was that it was the initial step that survivors needed to accomplish.

The name inherently implies survivors' first "push back" in their activism against the TTI that they needed to complete, which was to finally speak, voice their feelings, and tell their stories. The word "breaking" indicates and alludes to something seen as a violent gesture. It is an energetic action that vindicates our trauma. You can see it reflected in some of the early imagery of Breaking Code Silence, where a piece of tape is being ripped off a mouth. It is very full of emotion. That anger was undoubtedly a stage in my own healing as well. I view that anger as a necessary part of any movement, but it is still the first stage of activism and change.

I proposed naming the organization Unsilenced because we are no longer actively learning how to speak up. Collectively, for the most part, we are now outspoken, and we are going to continue to be.

It was a very intentional shift in the narrative to ensure we would be taken seriously. We shed the persona of angry, "troubled teens". For survivors to maintain a position of being angry, only serves to add to the confusion. When you occupy the fringes, you lose people.

You have to be able to collaborate with a lot of different individuals who not only operate in disparate sectors but may themselves be at different stages of awareness. You are much more likely to provide education to a more open and less defensive audience when you proceed from facts, not experiences alone. Or, to put it another way, a passion for the work is not the same thing as becoming overly emotional.

We have transformed into grown-ups who are ready to use our pain for purpose in professional ways to create the social change needed to stop institutional child abuse.

I had become attached to the idea of naming the organization Unsilenced, but I put it up for a vote, along with other options, to the volunteers, and the results were clear. Now, we were Unsilenced.

Community-Based Alternative

People ask me all the time, "Do you want to shut down the entire Troubled Teen Industry?"

I say, "No, I want to shut down the programs within the Troubled Teen Industry that have extensive patterns of abuse and operate without proper oversight and regulations."

Now, do I think any programs exist in the Industry that don't have abusive practices? Do any of them operate under the necessary oversight, regulation, and reporting practices and do they deserve to stay open? I think trying to retrofit this entire industry with the proper reforms and reporting is going to be a huge challenge.

In my opinion, with the TTI having roots in cult-based organizations, the long patterns of abuse dating back a century, and the lack of a real evidence-based foundation—all these factors make reform seem nearly impossible. Even if we eventually can instill proper safeguards within this industry, the "tough love" approaches, far-too-engrained social issues, and faulty belief systems still remain.

Until significant social change happens, the industry will continue to be dangerous for youth. However, policy work to reform the industry still needs to be done. It shows the world it is something we should care about, and it, along with the advocacy work, is helping generate that social change we need.

I understand that there are times when short-stay hospitalizations may be needed for times of crisis. Someone might need to go into inpatient so they can get the right type and dosage of medication to assist in stabilizing disorders such as schizophrenia or bipolar disorder. Other individuals may be having suicidal ideation and need genuine monitoring to make sure they don't carry that through. Those are acceptable reasons, provided the child is institutionalized for only the duration of the crisis, is overseen by medical professionals, and has access to advocates and support systems.

But, when you get right down to it, most kids are sent away for things that have very viable treatment options within their community.

One research study from Dr. Linda Wilmshurst in 2002 shows that 63 percent of at-risk youth treated at home had reduced symptoms of ADHD, anxiety, and depression, while only 11 percent had reductions of symptoms when treated in residential care. In fact, research also shows that youth who have close familial ties during their adolescence have mental health benefits, including lower levels of depression.

If we deduce from this study—and many others like it—that children fare better when they are within their communities, why don't we spend more energy trying to find community-based alternatives that afford families this option?

Most parents of struggling teens do not know even know community-based alternatives exist. Many such programs are underfunded and under-marketed. They are also more challenging to find; one approach might be available in one city but not another.

Parents don't really know what they are looking for. What should they type into their Google search bar? Alternatives to the TTI? It's hard for them to choose the alternative when they don't even know an alternative exists.

The programs certainly aren't going to tell them about other options that are available, or where to look. Treatment modalities can also be highly siloed. For example, there is a therapy, backed by research in treating at-risk youth, called Functional Family Therapy (FFT), which has been very successful within the juvenile justice system.

FFT is family-based therapy that doesn't focus on negative behaviors, it focuses on the strengths the family already has and motivates them to continue to build those strengths in ways that also increase self-respect.

Unfortunately, this intervention has historically been most commonly used in the juvenile justice system and isn't as widely seen in community health organizations.

My point is that there are so many alternatives to the TTI that exist, it is just about doing the work to ensure people are connected to them.

During my advocacy work I have connected families to alternatives that prevented their kids from being sent away, or gotten kids out of programs, or helped parents realize the trauma that was inflicted that led to them reuniting with their children. Advocacy work like this has allowed me to feel like I am healing that 15-year-old girl who is hurting inside.

Unsilenced has accomplished remarkable things in the areas of awareness, education, legal advocacy, legislation, transparency, and community support.

This work has also helped me become a better mom. It has made me a better wife. It has made me a better person.

Being the social change I want to see, has finally put me back in the driver's seat of my own life.

A Little of Our Work

Everyone at Unsilenced shares the collective mission of stopping institutional child abuse by empowering self-advocates to create lasting social change. We envision a world where youth are free from institutionalization, and the voices of young people are respected in the development of their own mental, emotional, and physical well-being.

Some of the most outward-facing impact we create in the area of preventing children from going into these programs is through Project SPEAK. Project SPEAK (which stands for Survivor Prevention through Education, Awareness, and Knowledge) re-educates the decision-makers in communities about the long-term effects of the TTI on youth.

We target multiple decision-makers in every pipeline such as juvenile justice, child welfare, foster care, school systems, and mental and medical health professionals. We provide the relevant facts that need to be in their hands before they make life-changing decisions for youths.

I never get tired of that look I see on people's faces when they wake up to what is really going on at many TTI facilities. They may still refer people to these programs, but at least they are doing so after a moment of pause to consider if there are better options.

It is important to note that during this education, we advocate for community-based alternatives to institutionalization.

Another area of our impact is our dedication to exposing the truth about this industry and helping survivors and their family find justice. Our Justice Support team strives to do this by conducting thorough investigations into both open and closed TTI facilities, bad actors, and the industry at large. We aim to facilitate opportunities for justice for survivors who were harmed in their programs by connecting them with attorneys who are able and willing to help them. Utilizing our access to a network of over 40,000 survivors, we maintain a nationwide youth congregate care database of survivors and their programs that allows us to identify potential plaintiffs, whistleblowers, and witnesses for current or future lawsuits.

We help these survivors break their own silence by helping them find access to justice, and then help embed those survivor plaintiffs into our therapist-led support groups and the community of survivors to help them feel emotionally supported as they are on that journey for justice. This team also conducts program-specific experience surveys to assess the treatment and practices at programs to help identify potential patterns of abuse, neglect, or maltreatment. They work on detangling what is an extremely incestuous industry.

Keeping tabs on the different programs and the staff who move between TTI programs is itself a full-time job. If someone gets convicted of child abuse in Utah and gets fired, what do they do? Maybe they'll move to Tennessee and get a job in another program? There's nothing preventing that from happening. Programs that are forced to shut down often simply incorporate under a different LLC, and they're open again. Due to a lack of communication between state agencies, it can resemble a constant game of whack-a-mole. Ensuring we always have the most up-to-date records from records request available for the public help us accomplish this.

Making sure survivors who leave their programs have access to their records is also incredibly important, as most times that is the only information they have from their life during that time, and that information oftentimes can validate their experiences of abuse.

We are also working on an IRB-approved research study through Baylor College of Medicine and the Menninger Clinic to better understand the impact of different levels of mental health treatment during childhood on people's outcomes.

Unsilenced believes in promoting transparency, and that is mostly done with a two-step process. First, our IT team maintains an extensive online program archive of over 100,000 documents and information on over 3,500 different programs. This is where we shine a light on the programs within the Troubled Teen Industry. Those documents contain DHS reports, police reports, media stories, survivor testimonies, and lawsuits. We are constantly finding things through the investigations team's record requests or online searches to add to the archive.

Everything that the IT and Justice Support teams have found is also put out to the public through our social media platforms by our Social Media team. Whether it is calling out programs and staff for abuse to create negative PR, elevating survivor stories, or pushing out Experience Surveys to the survivor community, the impact this causes is instrumental to our work.

Supporting survivors is at the core of our work and is woven through everything we do. We all collectively work to make sure we are giving back to the community in as many ways as possible.

We are approached constantly by survivors who are in the early stages of waking up or who are now out of the program and searching for help. These survivors oftentimes want to hold their programs accountable. They have a lot of questions, but because we aren't legal professionals, we knew we needed to create a resource to fill the gap. We started an Attorney Database that connects survivors to legal aid in order to hopefully help facilitate lawsuits that can lead to justice.

Survivors are now able to access that attorney database of law firms throughout the country and see all the attorneys in their state who are willing to litigate institutional abuse cases. Not only litigate but litigate on contingency, which is a huge deal for survivors. Many individuals who are fresh out of a program (or even later on) do not have the money to hold people or programs accountable. Hiring a law firm is extremely expensive and honestly a luxury for most people, survivor or not. The database is filled with attorneys who understand that survivors should not be responsible for payment until after abusers are brought to justice.

One additional survivor-focused area of impact I want to mention, is the donation of our Independence Packs.

Every year, youth in TTI programs "age out" by turning 18 and leaving the program. Oftentimes, due to stressful relationships that exist between youth and their families, many young people end up homeless and with no resources. Survivors that have this happen oftentimes not only deal with homelessness but also face a world that is very unfamiliar to them due to their seclusion from society.

We try to help address this by shipping packs to these survivors all over the country. The packs contain a backpack, laptop, gift card, and essential supplies to help support them during their journey towards stability. By providing resources to survivors who would have otherwise started their adulthoods with no support, we can empower them to reach their best potential as they reintegrate into society and begin their path to recovery from trauma.

Finally, we create a safe space for survivors to heal and connect with other survivors by offering free monthly support groups. This is something I personally had not seen occur prior to the arrival of Unsilenced in the community. I feel like the survivor community works so hard at trying to fight this industry, that they forget that they also need to take care of themselves.

Most of the incredible individuals within Unsilenced are survivors of Troubled Teen Industry programs. They do all of this work despite the scars they have from their youth. We also have some individuals who are allies, but regardless of what brought them here, they are all some of the most dedicated and incredible people I know. This group will change the world.

Helping Survivors Help Themselves

I have a confession to make. I am not just in this movement to help fight institutional child abuse. I am also here because I see a community that I really care for, feel connected to, and want to help. I am also here for all of them.

I get great satisfaction in knowing that a bunch of previously labeled "troubled teens" are all grown up now and facilitating social change against the industry that abused them. I get even more satisfaction knowing that the people in the movement, and this community as a whole, are some the best people I have ever known. It literally gives me chills.

Before founding Unsilenced, I had been told that survivors, on the whole, lacked the restraint or capability to do this work. I had no experience with the community yet, so I didn't really know better. "They're low functioning," a leader at Breaking Code Silence once warned me. In fact, the last thing I remember them saying to me before I left to start Unsilenced was, "This community is going to eat you up and spit you out, just like they did me." I think she was convinced that the community was so volatile, that because they didn't seem to be fans of her, they would never respect me. That really scared me to hear because, at the time, I didn't feel like I was a part of the community yet, and it allowed me to believe they could be a bunch of rabid dogs ready to tear me apart.

Survivors of institutional child abuse often struggle with CPTSD, and it is our defense mechanisms that keep us safe. We don't want to be told to trust anyone—that is exactly what got us in so much trouble in the past. So it is common for organizations in this space to fail. Yet I can, without a doubt, say that Unsilenced wouldn't be as successful as we have been without the community of survivors surrounding us, and the trust they put in us.

Unsilenced itself has (or has had) some of the most amazing people I've ever known. Some are still with us, and others have moved on to other parts of their lives. Our community and team members work tirelessly to fight for the youth in this country who are either unable to or too scared to use their voices and amplify the voices of survivors already speaking out.

While our mission at Unsilenced is clearly stated on our website, my personal mission behind the scenes is to help survivors help themselves.

Once thing that stands true for many survivors of institutional abuse is the additional challenges that exist in managing trauma disorder in "typical" work environments. While our culture has certainly come far in evolving into a trauma-aware society and understanding the effects trauma can have on individuals' lives, we have yet to see the full incorporation of this knowledge into employment practices.

Employers should know that survivors of institutional abuse suffer in a much different way than other trauma survivors they may have worked with in the past.

An employer may think, *Well, I have worked with survivors of natural disasters before, so I'm familiar with the challenges that trauma survivors face.* However, the reality is that while there may be some similarities between natural disaster-induced trauma and survivors of institutional abuse, anecdotally, we see far more differences than we see similarities.

I believe that survivors of institutional abuse tend to suffer much more often from CPTSD, whereas natural disaster survivors are seen much more often suffering from straightforward PTSD. The reason this occurs is likely because survivors of institutional abuse experienced prolonged exposure (for months to years) to a traumatic event. CPTSD can occur after ongoing emotional or physical abuse, neglect, or even being held captive. On the other hand, PTSD usually develops after witnessing or experiencing a stand-alone traumatic event. I believe understanding the similarities and differences between the two conditions, and how the conditions differ in treatment modalities is a much-needed area of research.

Due to the high prevalence of this CPTSD reported in the community, I think survivors of institutional abuse need a work environment that is exceptionally inclusive to counter the extreme limitations we were forced to live with during our time in the TTI. The flexibility to work from home part or fulltime can also be useful as survivors navigate the road to wellness and wholeness. This empowers survivors to work in an environment that provides positive adaptations suited to any potential neurodivergences, or any health or trauma-related issues that they might have.

Remote jobs seem to be much more conducive to survivors, as they allow us to be in control after not having authority for so long. When you have had dominion over you for as long as we had, you'd be amazed at the culture change you can achieve when you let survivors work from wherever they want.

Remote work also provides them with the opportunity to work from within the safety of their own home. Speaking for myself, this is the place I feel safest and it allows me to work in an environment with fewer triggers and more emotional safety. Most importantly, I'm in full control of my environment.

In a survey done internally within Unsilenced, we found that over 95 percent of respondents felt that we provided a safe place to connect to other survivors and work together as a team with a shared purpose. Furthermore, just over 86 percent of respondents found fulfillment in their own healing through their work with Unsilenced.

My goal, aligned with our organizational mission, is to expand and scale Unsilenced so that in addition to driving the essential societal transformation required to stop institutional child abuse we can also generate a multitude of job opportunities for survivors. This will enable them to engage in the advocacy work that could enhance their own healing journeys.

Chapter Twelve

AND JUSTICE FOR ALL

Waking up to the systemic dysfunctions and abuses within the TTI is hard to do. But it is not only TTI survivors who have to undertake the process. Waking up is also imperative for those in the education system, the lawmakers, religious leaders, and those in the criminal justice system.

Waking up is also a difficult yet important process for the parents of survivors.

Often, parents have a really difficult time accepting that a decision they made ended up hurting their kids. It takes deep emotional intelligence to take responsibility and accountability. As a result, oftentimes parents either deny the trauma that was inflicted on their child within a TTI program or maintain the stance that the child deserved to be sent away, regardless of the outcome. This can lead to the dismantling of relationships between family members and survivors in many cases.

I was fortunate enough to have parents who were willing to do the work necessary. It didn't happen all at once. My parents had to go through their own waking up experience, but it is something that I am so grateful took place.

After I had time to process things for myself, I started discussing my experience in the TTI with my parents.

One day, after a get together at my house, I was chatting with my parents at the kitchen counter and I said, "Chrysalis was abusive."

My mom responded, "Well, you got to be careful. That's a strong term."

In hindsight, I can see that their initial hesitancy came more from a lack of knowledge than denial. At that point, they didn't know what had gone on. I had simply phrased it in a way that would help me heal. I believe Kenny was abusive; that wording was initially too strong for them because they didn't have the information that led me to that point.

That first conversation sparked more over the next several months, whether on the phone, at my kitchen counter, or in my office. It gradually all spilled out.

I think our discussions were benefited by the fact that I was now in an emotionally healthy place, with a stable home and work life. By this point, I had found my journals and remembered so many details. I was able to ask them, "Did you know this happened?" "And this?" "And that?"

Their answer was always no. Every time one of those "did you know" questions was asked, I saw their faces become more and more panicked and frightened. Through these dialogues, they realized they, too, were manipulated.

I think that's when they started to go through the trauma of realizing that a significant decision they had made had hurt me deeply.

For example, they didn't know that throughout my time at Chrysalis I got into trouble for trying to get help for injuries and illness. They have dealt with so many of my medical emergencies in the past that when they heard about my inability to speak up about pain or conditions caused or worsened by events at Chrysalis, it created intense anger.

They do admit to having seen some red flags. My father reported, "It was interesting because when we came to visit you the first time at Chrysalis, I saw a girl sitting on the couch next to Kenny, and Kenny had his arm around her. I thought, *Is that weird?* Then I said to myself, *If I look at Mary to see how she feels about it, that will tell me.* I looked at her, and she was smiling, so I convinced myself it wasn't weird ...."

My mother said she always knew something was off about Kenny. While around him, she quickly caught on to how he played favorites and how toxic that was. Meanwhile, Kenny spoke about me in a derogatory manner to her from the beginning, and my Mom called him out on his attempt at manipulation after only a week of being there.

Kenny called my parents and said, "I don't know if she's going to make it here."

My mom told me she responded, "Excuse me? Are you saying I need to come pick her up?"

At this point, Kenny said, "No, no, no," and backtracked.

After that, Kenny made a point of stressing to them that I was doing well. He was likely afraid of halting the gravy train so he reverted to selling her on the merits of Chrysalis.

I find it hilarious that both my mom and I independently confronted Kenny on my first week there, albeit with much different results.

It Takes Years to Understand

There was a lot of emotion in those days of my parents waking up and coming to terms with the reality of my experience in the TTI. There were many tight hugs and direct apologies from both of them.

The actual apology itself is such an important step. It is much, much harder to forgive someone who maintains that they didn't do anything wrong and that it's all in your head.

A lot of survivors want an apology. In fact, they crave it, not so much so that their parents will feel ashamed, but because an apology solidifies and validates their feeling that they went through hell.

In this area, I have been blessed beyond measure. My parents are very involved now with Unsilenced. They come to my panels, advocate for change beside me, and travel with the organization in some of its outreach efforts.

My father even told his story through a megaphone on the lawn in DC, sharing his perspective as a parent who was led astray by the TTI.

After I posted a video of my father making this speech on to Facebook, I received several messages from survivors. They all said variations of the same thing: "That was extremely moving to hear your dad's story, and it caused me to reach out to my parents, and now we're talking."

During our first in-person fundraiser in November of 2022, my dad delivered the opening remarks to 100 people. His speech was both powerful and healing and I share it here.

> I thought it was best to lead off tonight by giving the perspective of parents faced with making tough but critical decisions about their child who is struggling and does not fit in ….
>
> Our hope for Meg growing up was for her to use her many gifts and talents to be a positive contributing member of society. Hopefully, you will see tonight that Meg has more than lived up to that dream.

However, the path for us to get here was not easy.

We have always felt, deep down, that we were blessed to have Meg as our daughter and teacher. All of us just somehow needed to successfully survive her teenage years.

Like so many parents of difficult children, our story is one of trying to figure out the underlying issues contributing to their child's difficulty to thrive, how we can be better parents, and how we can select the best schools and support their teachers.

Meg has always had many positive attributes. She is very bright, articulate, a truth-teller, and has a warm and compassionate heart.

Teenage Meg kept that warm and compassionate heart hidden and was also blunt and very strong-willed to the point of intimidating even the most confident adult. She was also very disruptive in the classroom. She unintentionally alienated her classmates, who, at that age, generally are not very tolerant of anyone different, and Meg certainly did not fit the norm.

Our struggle to help her included many diagnoses from numerous professionals, which included ADHD, anxiety disorder, oppositional defiant disorder, and bipolar disorder, among others, to "I just cannot figure it out."

As it turns out, only the first two were actually correct, and other critical diagnoses were missing. With advancements in genetics, mental health, and medical science, and a better understanding of the links between the three, coupled with Meg's determination to understand the root causes of her physical, and mental challenges, we now have a much clearer understanding of what we, her teachers, and, most importantly, Meg had been dealing with all these years....

We also now know she is on the autism spectrum. So, as it turns out, Meg's responses to her world as a teenager and what caused her to be labeled as difficult were both logical and largely predictable behaviors based on her genetics and conditions. Then, due to a lack of understanding and misdiagnoses, her behaviors were viewed as willful and correctable defects that the therapeutic boarding schools advertised they could fix.

When Meg was 14, after being told by numerous public and private schools that she would be "better off somewhere else," our family was desperate for help and turned to an educational consultant for guidance.

We made three critical decisions at that time that we regret now, knowing what we know today.

The first was to send Meg to a psychiatric residential hospital that treated the most extreme mental health cases. It was there that we were told that Meg was bipolar and needed a controlled environment or terrible things would result. They even told us that if left untreated, Meg would go on to have multiple teenage pregnancies with different men out of wedlock and would likely be addicted to drugs. This was very scary to hear as a parent, and only made us more fearful of not following through with the "experts" recommendations. This diagnosis and their predictions about it proved to be wrong, maybe with the exception of one conclusion, that Meg was the most formidable child this doctor has encountered in 40 years of practice.

The second decision, which seemed reasonable when suggested, was that we should *not* inform Meg ahead of time of our decision to send her to the hospital and to use an escort service to transport her there to prevent her from running away. We realized this was a huge mistake as soon as two off-duty police officers arrived at 3 a.m., telling Meg, "We can do this the easy way or the hard way," that she needed to get undressed and go to the bathroom with an officer present, and that they could not tell her where she was going. All we could do at that point was tell her repeatedly that we loved her and would not abandon her. It was traumatic for both of us, but frightening and devastating for Meg, having a permanent impact on her.

The third decision was to send Meg to a therapeutic boarding school with no real information about the program, verified results, evaluations from third parties or oversight agencies, and no information from parents or emancipating students. We now look back and wonder how we could make such an important decision without good information, but there was no other information available at the time, and we were desperate to get Meg the help we were told she needed.

At the time, all we had were the owners' claims—that they could successfully treat Meg's case and that they have a very high success rate, with one exception, "when parents naively listen to their child's complaints and remove them from our school early." We were warned against being one of those parents. Further, to minimize complaints from kids, we now know that calls and letters were monitored, and unfavorable comments were punished.

It has taken us years to understand the traumatic impacts of these three decisions.

I would like to conclude by saying my wife and I could not be prouder of Meg. She has harnessed her strong will and determination for good and has overcome obstacles that would have knocked down even the strongest person. As a result of a lot of investigation and hard work, Meg has become her best self; a terrific wife and mother of four children; and a purposeful leader. She continues to be our and others' teacher and our hero.

Her warm and compassionate heart is now visible for all to see.

Every Troubled Teen

When two individuals come through the way my parents have, it gives us all hope.

As you become an adult and possibly a parent, you are going to screw up all over the place. It's inevitable. But are you the kind of parent who is going to learn to say, "Thank you for explaining that to me. I had no idea that was happening to you, you must have been so scared. I am so sorry I made that decision. What do I need to do to help you through this?"

My hope is that this reunification happens in the lives of as many survivors as possible before it is too late. I don't mean to be morbid, but sometimes, it becomes too late. Sometimes, kids die. That's what happened to a 17-year-old girl, who we will call Rae, on December 20th, 2022, at Diamond Ranch Academy (DRA) in Southern Utah.

I have encountered many people who try to rebut my mission. They say things like, "Your experiences are 17 years old. That doesn't happen anymore. Programs have changed."

I wish that were true.

Instead, children continue to die every year, and every time they do, I am flooded with a feeling of helplessness because the industry is so huge. Each time, for a moment, I feel powerless.

When Rae died, I had a strong sense that I knew what had happened to her. I posted a TikTok that said, "Autopsy reports aren't back yet, but I am telling you right now, it is going to be some kind of medical condition that they ignored. Seventeen-year-olds don't just drop dead." It is almost like I knew what she had gone through, even before any reports were back. This caused me to feel especially connected to Rae because she easily could have been me. There were so many times when I was very, very ill and ignored.

Two things happened from that TikTok that I didn't expect. First, the video went viral, which prompted an influx of first-hand witnesses to reach out to me and confirm I was correct; Rae had been sick for weeks and denied medical care. Secondly, the video reached her family, and they reached out and asked for my help.

These two things led to Rae's family discovering the truth about what happened to Rae, which contradicted what the facility told them, and me discovering discrepancies in what was reported by DRA to the family regarding the timeline of her death.

I then connected Rae's family to Alan Mortensen, a Salt Lake City attorney who they engaged, and, over the next several months, Alan, Unsilenced, myself, Rae's family, and the entire community of survivors tirelessly worked to propel the community activism forward in hopes we could positively affect the case to hold DRA accountable and find justice for Rae.

The direct messages with information kept pouring in, so our investigations team, and myself developed a survey. We wanted to be able to capture the information that witnesses had to disseminate while also being able to see the bigger picture. We named it "DRA Experience Surveys". The survey for DRA got over 110 responses in a month and led to key information that helped us understand exactly what happened and helped entice the media to cover it.

This experience helped us realize the importance of what Unsilenced can offer law firms in this fight against institutional child abuse. We added expertise and knowledge to the case that only survivors could bring.

For instance, when the family received the box with Rae's effects and told me what was in it, I asked, "Wait a second, where are the journals?"

They said, "What journals?"

I said, "Every survivor has a journal. You're either forced to keep one or you need to keep one in order to survive. If there's not a journal in there, they took them."

And guess what? She did have a journal. I spoke to many witnesses that said she had many journals that never left her side. Isn't it interesting how those journals were not in her things that were sent back? Journals that, in my opinion, likely had copious amounts of information in Rae's own words exclaiming how sick she was and how no one believed her. How no one helped her.

Since the introduction of Experience Surveys with this case, we have now distributed fifteen similar surveys in the past nine months with over 971 participants. These surveys are a vital and valuable tool in gathering information from survivors and employees about the programs they attended or were employed by, allowing us to assess potential abuse patterns, collect employee names or incidents, and better understand facility environments to help direct our investigations into programs and their staff. This information becomes essential once we are alerted of litigation against a program and also allows us to inform survivors who wish to speak with attorneys and who may have crucial information.

Using the incredibly powerful voices of survivors, we have helped facilitate stories to come out that illustrated the deception of these programs, including their attempt to paint as accidental every death that occurs on a property.

Returning to Rae's case, when I was interviewed by news anchors for FOX they asked me, "What were your thoughts when you heard about Rae's passing?" I said, "The same thought I've had about every death—this was preventable."

It appeared to me that the extent of the lies in Rae's case went even further than that. I believe that DRA lied to Rae's family about how she died, but also when she died. There are even allegations that claim they may have said she was on her way to the hospital when in fact, she was already deceased. Thankfully, DRA was forced to shut down by the State of Utah when their license renewal was denied. I remember hearing of the closure while on a Zoom call with my friend, we both bawled our eyes out.

This program closure felt different from the rest. Historically speaking, Diamond Ranch Academy had its fair share of people trying to sue them and shut them down. But finally, after 24 years of operating and three deaths of children in their facility, they were done.

We cried for Rae, and we cried because we knew that facility wouldn't be harming or creating any more survivors. The abuse stopped with Rae and her peers.

A few days after the ordered closure, the Executive Director of DRA came out with a statement that didn't even mention Rae. Instead, he accused the state of Utah of not following correct due process and announced that the facility would close, effective immediately. They weren't even going to appeal the decision, which was a surprise.

Was he going to lease the property to another program that would be up and running in no time? Were they going to shuffle everything into a new LLC, in a different person's name, and have *them* run the facility? Due to the lack of regulations and oversight, programs do these kinds of things all the time. Did they close immediately because they were planning to sue the state later, and that would help them get a bigger financial settlement? It didn't take them long to attempt to apply for a license as a day treatment and outpatient treatment; they were denied that.

As of the writing of this book, the facility has already rebranded itself as "Rafa Academy" in the exact same building. In what I must assume was an attempt to throw people off their trail, they changed the street name of where they were located so that the address would look different on their website. However, if you go to Google Maps and search their address, you will see two facilities listed in the same place; Diamond Ranch Academy and Rafa Academy. As soon as we noticed it, our team began our work in yet another attempt to force accountability and foster awareness to this rebrand.

Rae's case has brought forth heightened awareness about the industry in Utah, and I hope it will bring even more regulation to close obvious loopholes being exploited.

Survivors of DRA would drive by the property and send me photos showing it was completely empty. One photo symbolically showed DRA's sign with their name fallen and shattered, with a giant crack running right through it. They left that sign much in the same way they left most survivors that exited; broken.

These things won't bring Rae back, though. Her family will have to deal with her loss every day of their lives. They are upset, frustrated, and destroyed. In the words of her father, "I thought she was sent somewhere safe to get help, and my daughter got sent home in a box."

Rae's passing away was a pivotal moment for me in this movement. We need to help parents and caregivers bring their children's cases to justice, and not just for those who passed away. It is one case among far too many where programs pull the wool over parents' eyes through false marketing and false promises. There is a stark difference between what caregivers think is going on in these facilities and what is actually occurring; both survivors and families are paying the price in that lack of transparency.

We also need to help parents every chance we get to seek out more direct, locally-based resources so they can still retain some oversight.

Right after Rae's death, I was speaking with a mother whose daughter was friends with Rae while they were both at Diamond Ranch Academy. After Rae's death, this teenager was transferred to a different facility. Her mother reached out to me to get more information about the program her daughter was sent to, so I informed her about it and told her about the industry. She cried when she realized she accidentally allowed her daughter to be a part of this industry.

I told her what I tell all parents when they are waking up. I said, "It isn't your fault at all, but it is also not too late to do something."

Then this mother said what I wish every parent would say when they hear about the abuse going on in the Troubled Teen Industry. In fact, If every parent with a child in a TTI program were to say what she said next, this industry would no longer be able to hurt children.

"That's it!," this mother exclaimed. "I'm going to get her out and take her home."

Epilogue

WHEN THAT TIME COMES

Recently, I traveled back to Montana. Sitting on the plane, I might have appeared calm, but inside I was that 15-year-old girl again, trembling and scared, who didn't want to take this trip but knew she needed to continue her journey. That girl had been scared to face her past for far too long. Every year had brought her more desperation and loss of control, begging and pleading for an older version of herself to help her feel safe and take away her fear. She wasn't listened to for far too long. Now I try to tell her she is recognized and safe. She is ready. I'm leading her down the path to take back Montana.

I'm wearing the Butterfly ring they gave me when I graduated Chrysalis. Despite my still having the same finger size, it feels tighter than I remember. My body instinctively knows it shouldn't be on my finger and keeps sending signals to my brain to take it off. It's telling me that my finger isn't getting any blood flow, that it's being strangled. *DANGER!* it screams at my brain. My brain knows better, however. It knows it needs to be there right now.

The reason I am traveling from California is to testify to the Montana State Legislature about the Troubled Teen Industry. It's been 19 years since my last testimony in this Senate building when I was still under Mary and Kenny's spell.

Back then, I felt so out of place, like the people in the room were so accomplished, and I was merely a child from the kid's table who was asked to join the grown-up party. This time was different. I not only deserved to be there—I belonged there. I was depended on to be there.

During the hearing, various senators asked questions regarding regulations and rules pertaining to a newly proposed bill. I was called up repeatedly as an expert to answer their questions.

Giving my testimony at that podium, I was speaking in the first person, but I knew I wasn't just speaking for myself. My words were for countless Montana survivors, some of whom never made it out of their TTI facility, some of whom are not able to live the life they desired or dreamed.

I imagined them standing all around me. One senator asked me whether this bill would be difficult for programs to enact and follow. Wouldn't it be micromanaging? He alluded to the fact that deaths can happen in any industry, such as foster care.

I waited for him to finish, then responded that any treatment, be it in hospitals or mental health facilities, should be based on outcomes—which is why places like hospitals are micromanaged. I told him that the parents with whom I've spoken, who have lost their child in TTI facilities, *wished* there was micromanagement going on.

His jaw dropped as he told me he had no further questions.

This is what becoming Unsilenced truly means—being vocal about what I went through and the changes needed. I didn't dissociate. I didn't go to Ben, who had accompanied me on this journey, for emotional support. When I felt anxiety, I accepted that I felt that way.

I felt gratitude that my voice was being allowed to speak for everyone, which took the ego out of it and simultaneously removed the fear.

I was glad Ben was with me for other reasons, of course. I was able to share with him where I went to college, so he now had a visual to accompany stories he had heard many times.

On the day we were to drive to Chrysalis, there was a white-out snowstorm, and we were in a front-wheel drive Toyota Corolla. I was grateful Ben was there to help me to decide if it was safe enough to proceed.

The road from Missoula goes along the continental divide, and it was white-knuckle driving the whole way. We felt like we had brought a feather to a knife fight, being able to see only 10–15 feet in front of us.

Maybe this was Mother Nature saying this isn't a trip we should take? But, no, somehow it felt fitting that we had to weather a big storm that tried to prevent me from returning to Chrysalis. Ultimately we continued because I ascertained that this wasn't a "sign" we shouldn't go, this was a manifestation of what Chrysalis represented to me coming out in the physical form. It symbolized what I endured in Chrysalis—how it was all so unexpected and chaotic and I was unprepared and unequipped with what I needed to survive and protect myself.

Somehow this little Corolla managed to let me guide it safely through the mountain, snow, and ice. Despite the elements, we emerged safely in Eureka, ready to embrace whatever came next.

It felt surreal to see Chrysalis again from the outside. When I went inside the main house to the dining room, however, I started to feel sick. Trauma had started to push to the surface, and I quietly acknowledged it within myself. I knew it was the 15-year-old part of me who was scared. I internally reassured her that she was safe, and that I wouldn't let anyone hurt her again. Once I acknowledged her fears, the feeling subsided.

I took in the long table where we had all once eaten dinner. The family dinner table usually symbolizes togetherness, sharing positive things about your day, but this table represented the essence of the dysfunction at Chrysalis.

The chair that Kenny once occupied seemed uglier and larger than the other chairs as if it knew what its role once was—as if it knew it once held the source of pain and trauma for so many children. Almost as if that chair somehow soaked up his narcissism and felt better than all the other chairs.

My gaze shifted to the usual spot where I sat. I remembered being called a pig there and having to eat my own vomit after throwing up vegetables I hated. I flashed back to all the years I spent trying quietly to edge my chair out of Kenny's eyeshot, praying my chair would do what Kenny's did; soak me up so I could simply just disappear so he didn't notice me anymore.

When I turned around from the table, I saw the living room; the infamous room where countless Circles took place. The room was trying to hide itself from me. Unlike the chair, this room was ashamed of what it had done. It had been completely redecorated. The carpet had been pulled out and hardwood floors put in. There were new couches, and the old tear-drenched ones were nowhere in sight.

But it didn't fool me; it was lipstick on a pig.

We all know what that room did. It stole people's self-worth. It created insecurities. It perpetuated trauma and, as aesthetically pleasing as it attempted to appear now, It didn't fool anyone.

The biggest surprise, however, during my tour of Chrysalis was how small it seemed in comparison to how I remember it. Perhaps that's because I was physically smaller when I went there, but I would argue it's because I have grown much bigger emotionally and psychologically than the limitations Chrysalis represented.

Seeing every nook and cranny now, I was able to ask myself, *Is this what you want to take up space in your brain?* And I was able to answer, *No, because I am so much stronger than them.*

I was ready to take back the identity that they had stolen from me.

After driving away from Chrysalis I also gave Ben a tour of the little town of Eureka. We kept our visit to town short as we were worried about another rough drive.

As good as it felt to enter Eureka, it felt twice as good to leave. I was leaving. Choosing to leave was a privilege I never had. I felt extremely free.

Miraculously, as if a smoke signal had been issued, alerting my surroundings to the healing that had taken place, I began to notice a discernible difference on our route back. Every previously icy road had melted, and all the treacherous conditions that tried to prevent me from reaching Chrysalis were now gone. There was no white-knuckle driving, only a light-handed touch on the steering wheel, as nature guided us back to the airport and then out of the state once again.

On that drive, I had an epiphany.

I am now daily living a life that I had accepted I would probably never have. There was such a long period of my life when if I had died at that point people would have said things about me like, "She had a really sad life. She was in a lot of pain. She suffered a lot." I think that was my worst fear back then. But that's no longer going to be the way people talk about me.

Now I know that if I died, it would be doing something I love, having an impact on people, and being part of a movement that has helped hundreds of kids and families. Now, whenever that time comes, I will die being proud of who I am.

I am Unsilenced.